2.24

AMOS, HOSEA AND MICAH

EPWORTH PREACHER'S COMMENTARIES

*

AMOS, HOSEA AND MICAH

*

NORMAN H. SNAITH
M.A., D.D.

LONDON : THE EPWORTH PRESS

THE EPWORTH PRESS
(FRANK H. CUMBERS)
25-35 City Road, London, E.C.1

SET IN MONOTYPE TIMES ROMAN AND PRINTED IN
GREAT BRITAIN BY THE CAMELOT PRESS LTD
LONDON AND SOUTHAMPTON

General Introduction

WE are living in a day in which the authority and message of the Bible are being re-discovered and declared. Preachers are realizing afresh that their message must be based on the Word of God in Scripture. Many commentaries on the books of the Bible are already available, and give much space to the consideration of critical questions and historical and literary problems.

This new series of commentaries, as its name suggests, is written specifically for preachers, and particularly for those who feel themselves ill-equipped to study the more advanced works of scholarship. Its aim is to set forth the essential message of the Bible. Questions of authorship, date, background, etc., will be dealt with briefly, and only in so far as they are necessary for informed preaching. The main purpose of each commentary will be (a) to explain the original meaning of each Biblical passage, and (b) to indicate its relevance to human need in the present situation. Bearing in mind this dual purpose, each author will have freedom to use what method of treatment he thinks most suitable to the book of the Bible on which he is commenting.

To save space, the Biblical text is not printed, but the commentary is based on that of the *Revised Version*.

This book, the third volume of the *Epworth Preacher's Commentaries*, has been written by Dr C. Leslie Mitton, who succeeded Dr Wilbert F. Howard in 1951 as lecturer in New Testament Language and Literature at Handsworth College, Birmingham. His outstanding gifts as scholar and teacher and his sound judgement and clarity of expression have already been shown, both in the lecture room and in his writings on the Pauline Letters. All who study this commentary will be stimulated, again and again, to preach from what Dr Mitton calls 'the most exciting of the four Gospels'.

GREVILLE P. LEWIS

Preface

IN his *Preface to the Epistle to the Romans* (1522) **Martin Luther** says of that epistle: 'It can never be read or pondered too much, and the more it is dealt with the more precious it becomes, and the better it tastes.' The Prophets are like that. I have grown through the years to be quite sure that Jeremiah is the best prophet of all, until I am reading Isaiah, and then it is Isaiah; but when I read Amos, it is Amos: and so it goes on —I wish we were all like that.

This little commentary is written to help preachers to think like that about Amos, Hosea and Micah. But the reader must do his own share of the work. To quote Martin Luther again: 'To begin with, we must have knowledge of its language and know what St Paul means by the words, law, sin, grace, faith, righteousness, flesh, spirit, etc.; otherwise no reading of it has any value.' This applies to Amos, Hosea and Micah. What exactly did they mean? What do the 'theological' Hebrew words mean? I have written this book to do my best to help preachers to understand what these words mean, so that please God they may see the 'bright light' (Luther again) which is 'enough to illumine all the Scripture'.

These prophets of the eighth century B.C. speak to us in the twentieth century A.D., and very much of what they said is strangely apt. They knew sin when they saw it, and they were pioneers to lead and guide men along the road to that Open Door by which 'if any man enter in, he shall be saved, and shall go in and go out, and shall find pasture'.

I think the abbreviations used are easily interpreted: to make sure: *RSV* is the new American *Revised Standard Version*; EVV means English Versions; *MHB* is the *Methodist Hymnbook*: *RV*m is the margin of the Revised Version.

May the LORD give the Word, and great may be the company of the preachers!

NORMAN SNAITH

LEEDS
5th July 1956

Contents

Amos

AMOS was a herdsman of Tekoa, ten miles or so to the south of Jerusalem. On the western edges of the barren, desolate wilderness of Tekoa, he tended his flock of short-legged sheep, moving to and fro from one sparse pasturage to another. But God called him to be a prophet, and he went north to Bethel, the royal sanctuary of Israel, the northern kingdom; there he prophesied doom and disaster to the prosperous north. And it was prosperous indeed. Just before the turn of the century (in 803 B.C.), Adad-nirari III had destroyed Damascus, the capital of the usually prosperous little Syrian kingdom. This left Israel without a rival, and Jeroboam II of Israel made the most of his opportunities. He reigned from 788-747 B.C., and Amos's prophetic ministry falls within that reign.

In the middle of this eighth century, Israel was wealthy and prosperous. But this did not mean that everybody was prosperous. There were great extremes of wealth and poverty, and the rich took every advantage of the poor; they oppressed them, and used the courts in order to screw every penny they could out of those that had no helper. This is the root of Amos's condemnation of Israel. The fulsome worship of the period, with its multitude of sacrifices and crowded shrines, was a 'false front'; behind it was every type of legalized lawlessness and immoral behaviour. The cult itself was riddled through with the immoral excesses of Canaanite religion, and Amos can see no future for Israel except the blacknesses of inescapable night.

The reader will notice that throughout the commentary, the three books, Amos, Hosea, and Micah, are divided into sections, and that each section is dealt with in entire independence of any other section. This is in line with the results of the modern study of the Prophets. It is generally agreed that the prophetic oracles are short, and almost always in poetic form. Often the poetic form varies from section to section; indeed, this variation is so marked in the Hebrew that it is a safe criterion for the separation of one oracle from another. It is evident that at one stage in the transmission of the oracles, attempts have been made at classification, so that oracles dealing with the same or kindred subjects are found forming a small collection. This is especially evident in Amos 1 and 2, and the same thing has occurred in the 'baker' oracles in Hos 7. For the preacher, this means that if he wishes to interpret his text by the context in which he finds it, he should certainly not deal with (say) more than the actual paragraph in Revised Version. Indeed, as the commentary shows, it is not always safe to use even the same paragraph for the context.

1^1: Introductory

The verse is in prose and is editorial. The rest of the book, except for the account of the clash between Amos and Amaziah at Bethel (7^{10-12}) and an occasional verse here and there, is poetry. The editor tells us who Amos was, where he came from, and what he did for a living. Amos himself later gives us a little more information (7^{14}). His sheep were *naqqads*—small and short-legged, but with abundant wool. The Arabs, however, thought little of them: 'Viler than a *naqqad*' is a term of great reproach.

1^2: The opening oracle

This is short and concise, like all Amos's oracles. It is well-suited to be a summary of his message: 'The doom is certain: the time is at hand.'

Follow *RSV* and read all verbs in the present tense. Read '*pastures*' (*RV* and *RSV*). '*The top of Carmel*' means the whole Carmel ridge, which ran south-east for twelve miles from the promontory by the sea—the scene of Elijah's victory (1 Kings 18)—toward Beth-shan, where the Philistines exposed Saul's dead body (1 Sam 31^{10}). In ancient times this was the most fertile tract of land in the whole country, and the last to suffer in time of drought. This is why it is mentioned here.

The doom is certain. When the lion roars, he is already leaping on the prey. The punishment is already in process; it is now inevitable and cannot be turned back ($1^{6, 9, 11}$, etc.).

In Deuteronomy generally, and in Ezek 18, the writers insist that every man must suffer for his own sin and that the righteous man does not suffer at all. The breakdown of this theory is discussed in the Book of Job, and is partly solved in Isaiah 53, where the innocent Servant of the Lord suffers for guilty Israel and by his suffering brings healing and health to Israel. Vicarious suffering, the innocent for the guilty, is the common lot of mankind. We are all bound together in one bundle (1 Sam 25²⁹) and all must pay the price of sin in varying degrees; there is no individual justice in this world except by accident, because there are no isolated individuals. But there is justice, strict, hard, inexorable, complete; not all our tears can wash out a line of it. God can deal with the guilt; He can clear it away so that the personal relationship is restored. But He does not do away with the penalty. In Christ, He shares it; He absorbs it. He shares it because He loves us with an everlasting love.

The time is at hand

This is a fitting motto for every oracle of the prophets. They all had a sense of urgency. It was this urgency which made them prophets. They had something which they were driven on to say by a divine necessity (cf. Jer 20⁹). The prophets believed that God is always active in His world, but at special times active with urgent, insistent power. These special times are the times of the prophets. The special urgency is due to the imminence of punishment for sin and of salvation for all who truly turn to Him (see 2 Cor 6²). Opportunity, the ancients said, is a swiftly running youth, his body slippery with oil, his head shaved except for a lock of hair on his forehead. He must be grasped by his forelock or never at all. The man who says 'No' now, will never have this present chance again, and he may never have another.

1³⁻⁵: The doom of Damascus

This is the first of a series of woes; there are eight in all, and all open with the same formula and follow the same general pattern. Some scholars see here general judgements based on general humanitarian principles. Others think that the oracles against Tyre, Edom and Judah are later than Amos (these are the ones which do not end with 'saith the Lord' or '*saith the Lord God*'). If these are later, the woes actually pronounced by Amos are directed against nations who have wronged Israel. The first is against the Syrian kingdom of Damascus. She must bear punishment for her brutal raids on Gilead—so brutal that they outraged the sentiment even of those rough days. The capital will fall, the royal palace be burned, and the Hazael dynasty wiped out.

For '*transgressions*' read 'rebellions', which is the true meaning of the Hebrew word.

For '*turn away the punishment thereof*', the Hebrew has simply 'turn it back', but the English translation is a correct interpretation. The Hebrews realized that punishment inevitably follows sin—so much so that the words for 'sin' often mean 'punishment' also (cf. Gen 4[13], where the margin shows that the Hebrew word is normally translated 'iniquity'). Most scholars alter the order of the four lines in **1**[5], and read 5*b*, 5*c*, 5*a*, 5*d*. Parallel thought and words form a notable characteristic of Hebrew poetry, and this rearrangement gives two excellent couplets, in which the parallelism is plain to be seen.

For '*inhabitant*', follow *RV*m, which gives an excellent parallel to '*him that holdeth the sceptre*'; cf. **1**[8], where a similar change should be made.

It is best to translate the words '*Aven*' and '*Eden*', and not to regard them as proper names. We then get 'the Vale of Wealth' (Damascus, which the Arabs call 'the world's garden') and 'the House of Delight' (? Hazael's palace).

The word translated 'rebellion' (**1**[3]) is the characteristic word of the prophets for 'sin'. To them, sin is not so much transgression from a path or the breaking of a code as rebellion against God. This is the basis of the evangelical conception of religion as a personal relationship with God. The primary thing for us is to get right with God, not to do what is right. Doing what is right, living a moral life, is necessary; but for the Christian these things must spring from a personal trust in God, and after this comes 'righteousness'. This righteousness is greater than that of the scribes (Mt 5[20]), and its demands are more than the barely ethical (Lk 17[10]); there is always an overplus, a doing of more than is required (Mt 5[38-48]).

1⁶⁻⁸: The doom of Gaza

Gaza and the other three survivors of the five towns of the Philistines are doomed because of their action in deporting a whole population into slavery. If the reference is to a recorded incident, it is probably that mentioned in 2 Chr 21¹⁶, a hundred years before the time of Amos and approximately contemporary with Hazael's savage raids on Gilead. The condemnation is not of the slave-trade as such, but of the wholesale removal of the population. The fifth town, Gath, was destroyed by Hazael (2 Kings 12¹⁷), and probably had not recovered by the time of Amos.

1⁹⁻¹⁰: The doom of Tyre

This oracle is probably a later addition, and is an adaptation of 1⁶. Tyre is charged with the same crime as Gaza and must bear the same punishment. The phrase '*and remembered not the brotherly covenant*' has never been satisfactorily explained in this Tyre context, and it is better to regard it as having originally belonged to the next oracle. Nothing is known of any incident which could give rise to the prophet's condemnation, and it is difficult to see in what way the non-Semitic Tyre could be a brother of the Semitic Israel.

1¹¹⁻¹²: The Doom of Edom

This oracle is generally regarded as a later addition, mostly because Israel, the northern kingdom, never had any complaint against Edom, and Judah's complaints belong to a much later time than that of Amos. In earlier times it was rather Edom who had just causes of complaint against Israel and Judah. '*Did cast off all pity*' is a free paraphrase of the Hebrew. The phrase looks late, and in that case could mean 'he destroyed his brother (born of the same womb)'. This could be followed by the difficult phrase of 1¹⁰, and the poetic couplets would then be complete in both places. When thus restored, the oracle tells the story of that rivalry between the twin nations, Judah and Edom, which is reflected in the stories of Jacob and Esau. Teman is in northern Edom; Bozrah was Edom's later capital (Isa 63[1]). The bitterness between the two peoples reached its height in the sixth century B.C. in the last days of the kingdom of Judah and in the first years of the Exile, when Edom made the most of Judah's national disaster. In 1[11], follow the Syriac and the Latin (Vulgate) Versions and read 'his anger he retained perpetually'.

The Edom which drew the sword will itself perish in sword and flame—cf. Mt 26[52], a saying which is true for every generation. Hate engenders hate; bitterness begets bitterness. The normal human reaction to wilful injury is retaliation. This increases the injury and the damage, and so the mountain of suffering and hatred grows. The effect is similar to a golf-ball bounding and rebounding in a narrow walled alley, except that the velocity of the rebound is increased every time. The Christian must absorb the suffering, and not retaliate. Thus only can the world's woes and hatreds be diminished. See 1 Cor 4[12], 1 Pet 2[23].

1[13-15]: The doom of Ammon

Here certainly is a genuine Amos oracle. Ammon rivalled Syria-Damascus in her brutal treatment of the Gilead-country, most of which at one time or another was disputed territory claimed by Ammon, Moab, Syria, and Israel. '*Rabbah*' (or 'Rabbath-Ammon', i.e. Rabbah of Ammon) was the capital. In 1[15], instead of '*their king*', some scholars read 'Milcom' (a word which has the same consonants but different vowels), the name of the Ammonite national god; it is better, however, to retain *RV*, *RSV*, and *AV*, because of the parallel reference to '*his princes*'. This parallelism of phrases is such a dominant feature of Hebrew poetry that it is, in the main, a good and safe guide to the proper interpretation of a passage.

2[1-3]: The doom of Moab

Moab is condemned because of the desecration of the bones of the Edomite king. We have no definite knowledge of the occasion on which this took place, but our information about the relations between these two peoples is so scanty that the reference may be some happening unknown to us. If it is a recorded incident, it will be the crushing defeat inflicted by

Moab on Israel and her two subservient allies, Judah and Edom, referred to in 2 Kings 3²⁷. The allies at first overran the Moabite countryside, but they had later to retire in great confusion and with considerable loss. That the victory of Moab was complete is testified by the famous Moabite Stone, which is King Mesha of Moab's own account of his successful revolt. This stone, with its ancient contemporary inscription, was found in 1868, after having been buried in the desert for over two thousand seven hundred years. There is a facsimile of it in the British Museum.

The bones were regarded in primitive times as especially containing 'life', and so possessing magic life-giving power. This was pre-eminently true of the bones of all sacred people, such as kings, prophets (2 Kings 13²¹), and so forth. These people in life, and afterwards their bones in death, possessed *mana*, that strange spirit-power to which primitive peoples have ascribed all unusual happenings and deeds. A survival of this ancient superstition is to be seen in the veneration of the relics of the saints and in the belief in their supposedly miraculous powers. To destroy a man's bones is definitely and finally to make an end of him (Jer 8¹⁻³). There are many passages which suggest that primitive peoples believed that as long as the bones survived, so did the man—even if they thought there was no survival apart from being a near-lifeless thing in the underworld. In Ezek 37, the dead bones of defeated Israel are dry and porous beyond hope, with no slightest suggestion of life in them; the magnitude of God's mercy and power is shown by the fact that He can quicken even the dead bones of lifeless Israel. God can give life, though man be dead (cf. 1 Cor 15).

2⁴⁻⁵: The doom of Judah

This oracle is not usually credited to Amos, mostly because the reasons given for the threatened disaster are far too vague and general for his vivid style. It is the vividness of his style and his mention of actual details that made him such a virile, up-to-date prophet. Contrast the dull generalizations of these verses with the detailed examples of 2⁶⁻⁸.

2⁴: '*their lies*' means 'false gods'. The same word is found in Ps 40⁴, and it probably has the same meaning there also, making an effective contrast between trusting in the Lord and turning aside to false gods. People become like the gods they worship, whatever these gods may be (Ps 115[8]).

2[6-16]: The doom of Israel

If we regard only the oracles which end with '*saith the Lord*' or '*saith the Lord God*' as being genuinely by Amos (and perhaps, too, even if we regard all the previous oracles as by him), then Amos hitherto has been making charges which would please every patriotic Israelite. But he suddenly turns now in full fury against Israel, the northern kingdom. Whatever crimes these nations have perpetrated, Israel has far outstripped them all, and this in spite of her greater privileges. It is as if a speaker should condemn the Americans of the slavery days on the basis of *Uncle Tom's Cabin*, follow it with criticisms of South African apartheid policy, and then suddenly turn and speak of the colour bar that exists in this country, usually showing itself more as we move higher in what is called the social scale. It is much more easy to condemn an action in other people and in other places than it is to see that same undesirable action in ourselves and at home; cf. Matt 7[3-5], where the Lord Jesus speaks of people who can see a speck of dust in the other man's eye and yet have a whole plank in their own.

Israel deserves complete condemnation. She has maltreated the poor, been guilty of immorality, and misused the holy shrines. All this is in spite of God's continued work on her behalf. He brought Israel out of Egypt, swept out the original inhabitants of Canaan, guided Israel through the desert, and provided her with spiritual guides in prophet and Nazirite. But Israel refused to listen to His word. Therefore punishment must come at last, swift and certain. Neither courage nor flight will avail in that day.

2[6]: Read 'sold up' instead of '*sold*'. The reference is to the harsh foreclosing of mortgages on the legal date and for the smallest amount.

2[7] is confused. Read '*that trample the head of the poor*' (*RSV*), but omit '*into the dust of the earth*', which is not a correct translation. *RSV* is making the best of a bad job.

2⁷ᵇ has occasioned much difference of opinion. The word '*same*' is in italics in *AV* and *RV*, which means that it is not in the Hebrew. It is best to think in terms of the English phrase, 'I go to the cinema', which does not necessarily mean that I always go to the same cinema, but that I go regularly to some cinema. The charge which Amos makes is thus against religious prostitution in general, a custom involving temple prostitutes and common to fertility cults generally. Deuteronomy 23¹⁷ follows the prophets in strongly condemning this sort of thing. It is clear that it was a Canaanite custom which was always creeping into Yahweh worship.

2⁸. For '*wine of such as have been fined*', read 'mortgaged wine'; '*clothes taken in pledge*' are either forfeited pledges or pledged cloaks not returned at night-time as the law demands (Ex 22²⁶).

2⁹. '*the Amorite*', according to Northern and Deuteronomic usage, is the pre-Israelite inhabitant of Canaan. Elsewhere it refers to the early inhabitants of the east-Jordan territory, allocated to Reuben, Gad, and half Manasseh.

2¹¹. '*Nazarites*' were 'consecrated' men who took special vows for a longer or shorter period and during that time allowed all their hair to grow long, shaving the hair both at the taking and at the discharging of the vow (Num 6). Cf. Paul in Acts 18¹⁸, and ancient Greek customs—e.g. Achilles when he went to Troy. They took vows also of abstinence, including abstention from wines and intoxicants. Like the Rechabites, they held by the ancient desert tradition and had as little as possible to do with Canaanite manners and customs.

2¹³ is difficult, and is probably a figure of speech from threshing, during which the wagon (a wheel is mentioned in Isa 28²⁷) pressed down on the floor full of sheaves. The picture of the harvest wain groaning under its load of sheaves belongs to the English countryside, though now out-of-date except in the Fenland; it is scarcely part of the ancient Palestinian scene.

The charges made here are not of illegal practices, of wealthy men breaking the law. Most of what Amos condemns was perfectly legal. His charge is that of making use of legal processes in order to 'skin' the poor. Legal conduct is not always

Christian conduct, and may indeed be a denial of it. The business men of Israel are using legal processes for their own purposes. They seek by sharp practices within the law to heap up fortunes and to live in luxury; they even use their gains in religious feasts (2^8). There is a type of man who 'uses' God, and seeks all the time to make capital out of his religion. Contrast *MHB* 446.

There is another type of man who holds that the precise fulfilment of the law is not only what is required of him, but is all that is required of him. He practises '*the righteousness of the scribes*' (Mt 5^{20}), the exact, careful and precise fulfilment of the Law. This is not the righteousness of the Christian (Mt 5^{38-42}, Lk 17^{10}). From the Christian an overplus is demanded, a righteousness which is more than justice. In Amos 'righteousness' is connected mostly with consideration for the poor. This is natural and indeed inevitable, because if a man is going to crusade for social justice, he must of necessity have most to say about that sphere where social justice is lacking, that is, among the poor and dispossessed. The effect of this in the Bible is that Righteousness has always a bias toward Salvation, toward helping those who have no helper. Indeed, by New Testament times '*righteousness*' can be equated with '*alms*'; cf. *RV* and *AV* of Mt 6^1, where some manuscripts read the one and some the other. There are passages in Jewish rabbinic writings where Righteousness is contrasted with Justice and means charity, benevolence, the doing of even more than justice requires. '*The righteousness of the scribes*' is the old legal righteousness; that of the Christian is in the true prophetic tradition, but enhanced and transformed by the righteousness of which Jesus speaks. Note Rom 1^{16-17}, where Paul states that there is '*a righteousness of God*' which is revealed in the gospel, which '*is the power of God unto salvation to every one that believeth*'. This '*righteousness which is of faith*' (Rom 9^{30}) involves those good works which God has prepared for us to walk in, the more-than-is-required, the overplus of the Sermon on the Mount.

3^{1-2}: Israel out of Egypt

The reference to the exodus from Egypt is of the highest importance. It was the beginning, and the outstanding example in Hebrew history, of that special knowledge which is

mentioned in 3². It is impossible to overestimate the significance in Hebrew history and religion of the rescue from slavery
in Egypt. This remarkable deliverance was the immediate
prelude to those stirring events on Mount Sinai whereby Israel
was called and sealed as the People of God. For ever afterwards, the Hebrews could scarcely speak of God and of His
ways with Israel without referring to His mighty saving deed
at the Red Sea. It was wonderful to them beyond belief,
because they were suddenly provided with a way of escape
when everything seemed lost (cf. 1 Cor 10¹³). This incident
fixed God in their minds firmly and irrevocably as being first
and foremost their Saviour God. They realized they owed
everything to Him, and that this was not because of anything
they were in themselves (Deut 7⁷, 8¹⁷, 9⁵), but because of His
mercy and His grace; no people on earth had been so favoured
and so signally blessed. Amos declared that such privileges
involve correspondingly greater responsibilities. Compare the
parable of the talents (Mt 25¹⁴⁻³⁰). The man who had made
no use of the one talent which had been entrusted to him was
cast out, and the man who had five was expected to produce
five more. It was not enough that Israel should be as good as
the surrounding peoples; the charge levelled against her was
that she was no better. Similarly, it is not enough that the
Christian shall salute only his friends. '*Do not even the Gentiles (AV, 'the publicans') the same?*' (Mt 5⁴⁷). The Christian
has received special favour; therefore punishment for failure
will be all the more severe (Jas 3¹).

The normal Hebrew word translated 'know' (see '*know*',
3²) can be used of any type of knowledge, but its characteristic
use is personal rather than intellectual. This is important when
we are thinking either of God's knowledge of us or of our
knowledge of God. The word can be used of the most intimate
of personal relations, e.g. Genesis 4¹ and frequently. It is
important that we should know facts about God, though we
cannot know Him fully in the sense of knowing all about Him
and understanding His thoughts and ways. But it is essential
that we shall know Him personally, be aware of Him personally, and there is a degree of fullness possible in personal
knowledge such as is not possible in intellectual knowledge.
It is because of this that we can '*know the love of Christ, which
passeth knowledge*' (Eph 3¹⁹: cf. *MHB* 52, 436). The result of
such personal knowledge is that we can '*be filled unto all the*

fulness of God'. Or again, to *'know him, and the power of his resurrection, and the fellowship of his sufferings'* (Phil 3[10]) is a matter of personal experience rather than of intellectual apprehension. These are things which we share in experience. A similar use of the word 'know' involving personal experience is to be seen in our common phrase 'knowing the road'. By this we mean that our knowledge is more than map knowledge; we mean that we have been over it again and again until we are fully acquainted with all its twists and turns, patches rough and patches smooth, and so on. This is the meaning in Psalm 1[6]: when the Psalmist says that *'the Lord knoweth the way of the righteous'*, he means that there is no step the righteous man takes but God is intimately aware of it. The classical statement of all this in the Old Testament is Psalm 139. (See also Isa 43[2]; 63[9]; Jn 10[14, 27]; 1 Cor 13[12]; and also *MHB* 387.)

3[3-8]: Cause and effect

The meaning is: if two men travel together, you can be sure that they have arranged it beforehand. If you hear a lion roaring in the bad-lands (not *'forest'* so much as rough country, full of all sorts of pitfalls and dangers, 2 Sam 18[8]), you know that he has leaped on his prey. If you hear a lion growling, you can be sure he has captured his prey. If you see a bird suddenly swoop down (the word means 'descend quickly' and not necessarily *'fall'*, cf. Gen 24[64]: *'lighted off'*. Omit *'in a snare'*) to the earth, you know something has attracted its attention. When the alarm is sounded in a city, you know that the people are terrified. When there is trouble, you must know that God is behind it. When the prophet speaks, you must know equally that it is because God has spoken to him.

Amos is justifying his message of 3[2], a message which must have struck his hearers as being strange. The popular idea was that a god is bound to take his people's part whatever they do; in the last resort he must save them for his credit's sake. This was the general point of view of other peoples (Num 14[16]), and doubtless of many Israelites also. As long as people thought this way, there was no possibility of any advance in moral and religious ideas. Amos's message is therefore of the utmost importance; it is the beginning of the prophetic emphasis on the significance of the fact that God chose Israel. If He did in fact choose Israel, then He must have existed before Israel, and equally He could exist without Israel. God is independent of Israel. He can and will punish her for her sin and disobedience. He can reject the people whom He has chosen. Morality is therefore of paramount importance, and so is the more-than-morality which grows out of the prophetic idea of Righteousness. God is not by any means compelled to forgive an Israel that is persistently wayward. In no way can it be said that God has failed if He rejects Israel. The modern equivalent of the popular idea that God must save Israel in the last resort for His credit's sake is to be found in a certain type of Universalism, which can be interpreted to mean that God is bound at last to forgive all men—a type of Universalism which definitely involves a doctrine of purgatory.

3⁷ is generally regarded as an addition. If it means that prophets have a monopoly of the knowledge of the purposes of God, then the statement is as false as the declaration that priests have this monopoly. If the meaning is that God is pleased to reveal His secret plans to the prophets in order that men may be warned (Ezek 3¹⁷⁻²¹, 33³⁻⁹) and repent, then the statement is sound.

3⁹⁻¹³: The doom of Samaria

This section is of mixed metre, and probably consists of three separate fragmentary oracles which have been dovetailed together so as to make a coherent whole.

3⁹⁻¹⁰. The prophet calls upon the near-by heathen to witness the oppression which is to be seen in Samaria, the capital city of the northern kingdom, Israel. The rich are storing up in their palaces the proceeds of their violence and rapacity. Some scholars wish to change '*Ashdod*' to 'Assyria', following the Greek Version (the Septuagint), but it is best to follow the harder reading. It is easy to see why a change may have been made to 'Assyria', because combined references to Egypt and Assyria are very common; it is hard to see why any scribe should make the change to Ashdod. To a herdsman of

Tekoa like Amos, however, Ashdod and Egypt were the two nearest neighbours; for his activities consisted of watching sheep in the southern highlands and tending sycomores (see note on 7¹⁴) in the hills bordering on the Philistine country.

3¹¹. The punishment is bound to come, and the God of Israel '*shall deliver the needy when he crieth; And the poor, that hath no helper*' (Ps 72¹²). The disaster will be so complete that scarcely one survivor will escape.

3¹². Here, though the Hebrew text is difficult and uncertain, it is better to follow *RV*, with its picture of the rich oppressor cowering in the corner of his divan, in the day when the '*palaces shall be spoiled*'.

3¹⁴⁻¹⁵: The doom of Bethel

The disaster is extended to the royal shrine at Bethel, where even the altar-horns, the most sacred parts of the altar, will be destroyed. The wealthy people built winter-houses for the cold rainy season and summer-houses for the hot rainless one; both will be smashed down.

3¹⁵. For '*great houses*', read 'ebony-houses', i.e. houses panelled with ebony, similar to '*the houses of ivory*', which were panelled with ivory. Ahab built a famous ivory house in Samaria (2 Kings 22³⁹, Ps 45⁸), and it is evident that he set a fashion for the luxurious nobles and merchants of succeeding generations. See also the notes on 9¹⁻¹⁰.

4¹⁻³: The doom of the fine ladies

Amos is fierce against the fine ladies of Samaria, who make such demands upon their husbands that, in order to gratify their wives' fancies, they oppress the weak and bully the poor. But the days will come when these women will be carried out in large shields and their posterity in fish-pots—taken straight out through the breaches in the walls and cast on the dung-heaps.

4³. The Hebrew has apparently *'into Harmon'*; many suggestions have been made to solve the mystery of this word, but 'dung-heaps' seems the best guess. Half the ancient Versions favour the rendering of *RV*—*'hooks'* (through their noses, like ringed bulls) and *'fish hooks'* (? through their posteriors). In any case, the final fate of these dainty women is intended to be coarse, brutal and ugly, in stark contrast to the selfish luxury which had characterized their living days.

4⁴⁻⁵: Empty religion

The prophet is attacking the empty show of a scrupulously correct ritual which has no real religion behind it. He is not against the local sanctuaries at Bethel and Gilgal, for the law of the One Sanctuary came over a hundred years later. *RV* and *RSV* insert *'every'* twice in 4⁴, probably intending the passage to mean that the people brought their tithes every three days instead of on three days in the year, and suggesting that they were offering far more sacrifices than was necessary. But it was perfectly proper to bring a morning sacrifice every day, and perfectly proper to bring tithes three times a year (the Hebrew need mean nothing more than this). It was perfectly proper to bring a thank-offering which had no leaven in it (read 'without leaven' instead of *'of that which is leavened'*), and perfectly proper also to declare their vows so that others should hear. Amos ironically encourages them in their exact and complete performance of ritual detail. They like doing it; it pleases them. They like people to hear them making vows. It is as well that somebody is pleased with this sort of thing, because God is not interested in it. Amos calls all this rebellion against God. It is sin.

To make a parade of religion is easily recognized as being very wrong (Mt 6¹⁻⁵). It is possible also to find one's own satisfaction in religious exercises: thus in Zechariah 7⁵⁻⁶ the prophet criticized the fasts of the fifth and the seventh months, which had grown up in the seventy years of the Babylonian exile, because the people found satisfaction for themselves in their fasts; they were thus not true fasts to God. It is wrong to regard ourselves as acquiring merit by the precise and exact fulfilment of religious rites. It is equally wrong to seek aesthetic enjoyment in the worship of God. It is equally wrong to find personal satisfaction in the absence of precise ritual or of aesthetic considerations. Worship is seeking God for Himself alone; it consists of humble devotion and true piety of heart. Any parade, any self-satisfaction, any pride of performance is rebellion against God; there is no true worship. Such conduct is serving man, serving oneself; but it is not serving God. It is good that all things should be done decently and in order, but never at the expense of the free functioning of the Holy Spirit. It is good that there should be offerings to God, all the offerings of every type that man can devise; but what God fundamentally requires from every separate one of us is repentance and faith. Without these, nothing counts, nothing is of any avail. Without these, all gifts are gifts to ourselves, and not one of them is a gift to God; they are all sinful.

The custom of taking a tithe is very ancient, and it provides a good basis for a Harvest Festival sermon on stewardship. The custom was followed by many ancient peoples. It is not mentioned in the earlier Hebrew codes, but it was evidently well established by the time of Amos in the eighth-century B.C., and it is mentioned in 1 Samuel 8^{15} as being illegally used by the king for the maintainance of his entourage. There was an annual tithe of field and fold (Deut 14$^{22-3}$), and every third year this tithe was given to the poor (Deut 14$^{28-9}$). This poor-tithe was probably an innovation of the late seventh-century B.C., and was part of the general new legislation of King Josiah's time designed to alleviate the distress of the depressed classes. The original custom appears to have been to take the tithe to the nearest shrine and there to hold a sacred feast; but with the introduction of the law of the One Sanctuary in King Josiah's time, the law had to be modified. The actual tithe could be sold locally, and other food bought at the Sanctuary with this money. The Levites were admitted to this tithe-feast (the original of the Harvest Supper), and this element developed until in post-exilic times the whole of the tithe was allocated to the Levites. But the tithe at all times was sacred and had to be eaten on holy ground. In this way it partook to some extent of the nature of first-fruits, which is what our harvest gifts today actually are. Presumably in early times, the first-fruits were taken out of the tithes. It is good to remember that all harvest gifts are holy, and that they are God's gift to us rather than our gift to God. The theory of first-fruits and tithes is that all produce of every kind belongs to God and is originally holy. This applies to produce of field and fold, beast and man. We must bring to God at the shrine the first-fruits and thereby acknowledge that all the increase is His. He then permits us to use the rest; but that remains His, and must be used according to His good pleasure and what is well-pleasing in His sight. Among the Jews, no first-fruits of the field could be redeemed; it went for the maintenance of the post-exilic priesthood. The first-fruits of cattle and sheep could be redeemed at a statutory redemption price; if it was not redeemed, it went to the priests. The first-born of the ass could be redeemed; if it was not redeemed, it had to be strangled. The first-born of man had to be redeemed at the stipulated redemption price. The theory of first-fruits and the original theory of the tithe is a lesson in the stewardship of property and even of human life itself.

4⁶⁻¹²: Ye have not returned unto me

Here is a series of five short oracles, all in the same general pattern and all ending with the same formula. The conclusion is *'prepare to meet thy God, O Israel'* (4¹²). Israel has suffered five major disasters: famine, failure of the October rains, blight, plague, and general ruin. The prophet sees all these as repeated calls to repentance. Israel took no heed and did not turn back again to God. Therefore (4¹²) the judgement is at hand; the price of continued sin must at last be paid. In modern days, when so many people think of God as a God of love in such a fashion that He is bound to give men opportunity after opportunity for repentance in an unending succession, it is well to remember such passages of Scripture as this (see also Mt 25¹⁻¹³, Mk 13³⁴⁻⁷). There comes a time when the door is shut. There comes a time when the Word of God is *'Prepare to meet thy God'*.

The five disasters are all due to what we today call natural causes, what the insurance companies curiously call 'acts of God'. To what extent is it proper and right in these days to ascribe such disasters to God in any personal sense? Most of us in these days would not ascribe such happenings to the direct action of God. We should ascribe them to God only in so far as they are incidental to life in a world which God has made. The Hebrew prophets tended to pass over secondary causes and to ascribe such things directly to God. They did this partly because they refused to acknowledge any other superhuman agency; since every event must be caused by a person, and since these events were obviously not caused by any human being, obviously they must be caused by the only other being that exists, that is, by God. They did it partly also because they were so very sure that God is intimately near. They knew that God's thoughts are not as our thoughts and that His ways are not as our ways (Isa 55[9]). They knew that God is transcendent in His nature (cf. Isa 40), and that in this respect there is a great gulf between God and man. But this did not prevent them from realizing that He was near to them. Indeed, the Unknown Prophet of the Exile (Isa 40-55) is at one and the same time the prophet who has most to say about the transcendence and uniqueness of God and the prophet who most insists on His immediate nearness; the author of Isaiah 55[9] is the author of Isaiah 43[2-3]. God is not man, but He is in our midst (Hos 11[9]). This consciousness of the nearness of God and belief in His immediate action as Saviour led them to ascribe all natural disasters to Him also. The modern age, with its scientific achievements and its consequent ability to explain the immediate causes of many events, encourages us to think of God as having little to do with this world in which we live. God has become as remote as Aristotle's Absolute, that God of much Catholic theology who is so remote that there must be intercessors between Him and us. God has become remote even in much Protestant theology, and any work of salvation He accomplishes, indeed any action of His of any type, is thought to belong to some world other than the world of our senses. It is essential that we find some middle way here, recognizing on the one hand the ability of science to trace causes and effects in the physical and psychical worlds, and at the same time realizing that God is near, deeply concerned with what we do and are, and is Saviour in small things as well as great, in material as well as in spiritual realms.

All happenings can be divided into three classes. First, there are the events which are due to the cut-and-thrust of living in a free world in which all living things have to fight for their own existence and for the future of their progeny. Illnesses due to infection and contagion come under this head.

If man is to survive, it must be by fighting and conquering other forms of life, and there is, in general, no particular moral reason for the incidence of these illnesses, apart from those which are definitely due either to immoral behaviour or to bad conditions caused by human greed or ignorance. All such events are neutral so far as God is immediately concerned. Included in this category are all true accidents and all tragedies which result from man's attempt to understand and to harness the forces that are hidden in the world. They are the price we have to pay for the mastery of the earth, and God has nothing to do with them in any direct way. The problem is not wholly resolved of course, because if God made the world, He either deliberately made it this way, or else the world has in some sense '*turned its own way*', and in each case we are faced with a dilemma. Second, there are troubles which arise because of man's misguided attempts to order the the affairs of this world. We have to order these affairs and cannot avoid the responsibility. Our mistake is that we seek to run the world the wrong way. We Christians believe that God has made this world so that it can be run in one way only, and that is His way; all other ways end in trouble and disaster. There is an inherent rightness in things, and whoever tries to order life on any other basis than the way of God will bring trouble and disaster on his fellows. This way of God, the Christian believes, is not any merely moral way, however excellent; it is the way of Christ, with all the overplus and the more-than-is-required. There is no other way. If Amos had been a prophet in modern times with a knowledge of modern science, the likelihood is that he would have used such incidents as come in this category to provide his illustrations—examples of those laws of cause and effect which apply to the way in which God has made this world. He would have referred, as the product of human selfishness and greed, to the suffering caused by war, or to near-famines caused by manipulation of the world's food markets, or to the poverty and hunger resulting from the devaluation of currency which is itself caused by non-co-operation between nations, or to the want which is due to the raising of tariff barriers, or to the misery which follows from class and race distinctions—all of them the results of attempting to organize human society in other ways than God's ways, and all of them causing further and further distress. The third kind of happening consists of human deeds which have their origin in the direct guidance of the Holy Spirit; this is the chief kind by which God directly influences the affairs of men.

4[13]: A doxology

The Book of Amos contains two or three of these sudden rhapsodies or doxologies. It may be that Amos himself suddenly bursts forth in a panegyric or in praise of God, just as Paul does in his epistles (Rom 11[33-6]). The general opinion, however, is that here we have a later insertion. The argument is that a piling up of phrases of this type is not the normal style of this prophet; the matter and the phraseology are exilic or early post-exilic. Further, there is a tendency to insert such panegyrics into prophetical writings, as can be seen in the Greek Version (Septuagint) of Hosea 13[4], where a similar passage is to be found. The word translated '*thought*' is otherwise unknown, and the ancient Versions all guess at its meaning, rendering it as glory, works, declaration, and even Messiah (Greek). The best solution is to take it to mean 'intention', and to interpret the phrase to mean that God declares His ways to the men of vision who can see something of His plans for man and can therefore declare them to mankind.

5[1-3]: Two laments

Here we have two laments, each with a short prose introduction. The laments consist of 5[2] and all of 5[3] except the first five words. They are in the famous 3:2 rhythm, a line of five accented words with a division after the third. This produces a peculiar halting effect. It is the metre of the *Qinah* (lament). The first lament is for Israel, hitherto unconquered but now doomed to fall. The second is for cities that mustered a thousand men for war and saw only a hundred of them return, or who sent out a hundred and lost all but ten. They are prophecies of that complete disaster which Amos believed to be imminent and unavoidable, a punishment for Israel's persistent apostasy.

5[4-6]: Godless shrines

Amos here for the first time deliberately attacks the provincial shrines, singling them out by name—such time-honoured sanctuaries as Bethel, Gilgal, and Beer-sheba. In 4⁴ he has attacked the sort of worship which pleased the worshippers and amounted to nothing more; here he attacks the whole system at the shrines, and denies that there is any worship of God there at all. His attack is not based on any theory of the One Central Sanctuary, such as we have in Deuteronomy; he is against the shrines because of the type of worship practised there. Again, he is not against the calf-worship at Bethel as such, but against false religion everywhere. The fact that a shrine has been hallowed for centuries is no guarantee of its present holiness. Bethel had been a sacred site, according to Hebrew tradition, ever since Jacob was benighted there as he fled from his brother Esau. Probably it had been a sacred site long before that day, for sacred sites are not invented so muc as taken over by the new religion. The story of Beer-sheba goes back to Abraham, and Gilgal had ancient associations with Joshua and the entry into Canaan. Ancient memories, ancient forms of worship, ancient traditions, ancient buildings— these can all become dead and can lead men away from God instead of to Him. All worship everywhere, at every holy place, must be kept alive by present-day, immediate knowledge of God. When men seek a shrine just because it is a shrine, when men worship for worship's sake, they are not seeking God. An attachment to bricks and mortar is no substitute for religion; it is as far away from true religion as an attachment to any particular form or ceremony. The one thing that con-stitutes a holy place is the actual worship of a holy people, a people that has a 'lively faith'.

5⁷, ¹⁰⁻¹³: Corrupt courts of law

These five verses may be a series of fragments, but the metre is substantially the same in them all, and so is the subject matter. Verses 8 and 9 are an intrusion, a panegyric of the same general pattern as that in 4¹³; they can be fitted into the context only by the arbitrary insertion of '*seek him*' (5⁸). Amos condemns those who dispense justice so as to leave bitterness behind, those who destroy true justice and hate the honest witness. They trample the poor and take from them load after load of corn; they bully honest men, take blood-money, and defraud the poor man in the courts. They are using the courts in order to oppress the poor, and they are taking advantage of every law process that money can provide. The best thing a prudent man can do is to hold his tongue. Amos calls all these sharp practices 'rebellious acts'. The English versions all have '*transgressions*' (5¹²), but this is an error. The prophets think of such actions, not so much as transgressions of a law, but as rebellions against God (see the note on 1³). His complaint is not that the actions of these men are illegal. They are perfectly legal. These men actually obey the law, but they use it to oppress the poor. There is something more demanded than that justice which is the strict observance of the law. We have something more in our English courts; we call it Equity. For the Christian, there is still something more, the way of Christ, where the ultimate concern is the positive reclamation of the guilty; to use Old Testament terms: '*Have I any pleasure in the death of the wicked? saith the Lord God: and not rather that he should return from his way, and live?*' (Ezek 18²³).

5⁹, ⁸: The mighty God

Verse 9 as it stands in the Hebrew is untranslatable, and verse 8 can be brought into the context only by inserting '*seek him*'. If we make two slight changes in two letters, and transpose the two verses, we get: 'He that causeth Taurus to gleam after Capella, and makes Taurus set after the Grape-gatherer, the Maker of Pleiades and Orion, He that turneth pitch-darkness into morning, makes day darken into night, calleth aloud to the waters of the sea, and has poured them over the surface of the earth, the Lord is His Name.' We thus have a doxology in praise of the God who controls the constellations in the sky above and the rains on the earth below. Capella the Goat rises at the end of April, and Taurus the Bull in May. The Grape-gatherer (Vindemiator in the constellation Virgin) sets in September.

5¹⁴⁻¹⁵: It will soon be too late

The phrase '*the remnant of Joseph*' can scarcely be earlier than 733 B.C., the year when the northern provinces of Israel were overrun by the Assyrian king. Possibly it is later than 722 B.C., when Israel was utterly overwhelmed and ceased for ever from being a nation. The verses therefore are a call for a

last-minute repentance. There is a chance for the survival of
what is left, but an immediate and sincere repentance is
essential. This repentance involves a complete change of heart
and life; nothing short of this will avail. The people say that
God is with them. If they truly turn to Him, then what they
claim will be true.

Some people are troubled about death-bed repentances.
They say that it is not fair for a man to repent at the last
minute and find his way into heaven on the same terms as they
themselves who have been Christians for years. There are two
things wrong here: one, it assumes that the unrepentant sinner
has a better time in this world than the Christian, and that the
Christian has missed something worth having because he has
been a Christian; two, it assumes that the merit of good works
is what qualifies a man for heaven. Concerning the first point,
there is no need for any further comment. Concerning the
second, it must be reiterated that '*by grace are ye saved
through faith*' (Eph 2[8])—by grace alone, and through faith
alone. It is 'by grace alone' because everything from first to
last depends upon the grace of God, that full, free, unmerited
love of God which streams out to all in a mighty river that
none can check. It is, from our side, 'by faith alone', because
our faith is the one thing that is still left. God, by His grace,
has done all that can be done from His side. What remains is
that every separate one of us shall turn to God in true, humble
penitence of heart, in complete and absolute trust. Subse-
quently, as long as this earthly life lasts, we must, still by His
grace, produce the fruit of the Spirit (Gal 5[22]). It is required
that men and women should be growing Christians all the
time, and not be always '*babes in Christ*' (1 Cor 3[1]). Some
people are always being converted, and profess conversion
again and again at evangelistic meetings. This is not good;
they are enjoying only the first joys of Christ—those elemen-
tary delights of the Christian life which indeed have their own
charm and rapture, but which are 'beginner's joys'. The
Christian must grow up; he must '*grow in the grace and
knowledge of our Lord and Saviour Jesus Christ*' (2 Pet 3[18]).
The people who can be effective witnesses in this world to the
saving grace of our Lord Jesus Christ are not the immature
Christians who know and desire nothing more than the thrills
of conversion; they are the Christians who have passed on
from that experience and are by way of growing '*unto a*

c

*full-grown man, unto the measure of the stature of the fulness
of Christ: that we may be no longer children*' (Eph 4[13]). Good
works that are grounded in faith are increasingly demanded of
the Christian all his life long. It is nevertheless true that for
all, whether newly converted or having grown in grace and
faith, it is only by His grace that a man can at any time, and
on either side of the grave, be in Christ.

5[16, 17]: Woe upon woe

After the usual prose introduction, we have three *qinah*
(lament) lines, with their halting rhythm designed to express
the extremity of woe. There will be lamentation and sorrow
everywhere, in town and country, and by amateur and professional. The God who comes with mercy and forgiveness
for the repentant is the God who comes in judgement for the
wicked and unrepentant.

5[18-20]: The Day of the Lord

These three verses contain one of the most important and
revolutionary things that Amos had to say. '*The Day of the
LORD*' is the day when God puts everything straight and all is
well for ever and ever; it is the beginnning of the millenium, the
day when all will be light, the day which all men desire. Amos
says that when God puts things right, it will be a black day
for Israel, total darkness without one redeeming ray of light.
When the Lord puts things right, it will be righteousness that
will rejoice and be on top; evil, apostasy, rebellion against
God—all these things will be cast down, because '*the LORD
alone shall be exalted in that day*' (Isa 2[12]). A wayward,
unrepentant, apostate Israel will be overthrown in company
with all that is alien to God. There is some difference of
opinion as to the origin of the phrase '*the Day of the LORD*',
but the best explanation is that the phrase originally referred
to New Year's Day, the opening day of the Great Harvest
Feast which began with an all-night festivity on the night of
the Harvest Full Moon. Many scholars think that this festival
included ceremonies extending over a number of days, including processions, liturgies, and possibly enacted myth-stories in
which the Coronation of God was observed in the ritual every
year; He took His seat once more on His heavenly throne and

decreed the fate for the new year. However all this may be as to its detail, there is no doubt about the fixing of the fate.

They expected salvation to come at the end of the year: *'the harvest is past, the summer is ended, and we are not saved'* (Jer 8²⁰). All peoples expect a change of fortune with the change of the calendar. Israel was in this respect like the rest, and they went farther; they looked for God so to restore the fortunes of Israel on one greatest day of all, when all would be prosperity and happiness for ever. Amos declares that a wayward Israel has no future, and that when the Great Day comes, there will be no hope for her. Further, there can be no possible escape from the darkness of the national disaster. He gives a vivid picture of a man running for all he is worth from a lion, seeing a bear ahead, dashing back, and just managing to slip into his own house, where he leans exhausted with his hand on the wall, only for a snake to bite him fatally.

The choice before a man is always being presented in the Bible. *'I have set before you life and death, blessing and cursing'* (Deut 30¹⁹). *'How long halt ye between two opinions?'* (1 Kings 18²¹). *'The wages of sin is death, but the free gift of God is eternal life in Christ Jesus our Lord'* (Rom 6²³). *'It is a fearful thing to fall into the hands of the living God'* (Heb 10³¹). See the closing verses of Ezekiel 18, where there is one of the most impassioned pleas for man to repent and turn to God found anywhere in the Bible. Many people, in their idea of fatherhood, have revolted from the stern father of Victorian tradition and turned to the often indulgent parent of today who refuses to check or discipline his children. With this has developed an idea of a God who is all tender love and no stern judgement. But He is both full of love beyond any human estimation as to content and quality, and stern in judgement, insistent upon repentance. It is His purpose that all men shall be saved, but only on the condition that they have repentance and faith. There can never be reconciliation between man and God on any other terms. The choice is plain and clear throughout the Bible; God is loving to the sinner, but His face is stern to the unrepentant.

5²¹⁻⁷: Away with feasts and sacrifices

God rejects the whole of Israel's worship, all her big festivals, all her sacrifices, all her songs and music. There was nothing of this in the good old desert days. Israel can take her idols away with her into captivity beyond Damascus.

5²¹. The '*feasts*' were the three pilgrimages, the harvest festivals of Palestine—Unleavened Bread, at the Spring full moon, which was the barley harvest festival; Weeks, seven weeks later, which was the wheat harvest festival; and Ingathering, at the autumn full moon, which was the vintage harvest festival. All these were Canaanite feasts, being closely tied to the agricultural years. Amos is right in saying that there was none of this in the desert; they do not have any place in the pastoral life of shepherd nomads. The word translated '*solemn assemblies*' means 'closing assemblies', the celebrations on the last great day of the feast; once more, there was nothing of this in the desert.

5²². '*burnt offerings*' were offerings which were completely burned on the altar, wholly a gift to God. In post-exilic times, '*meal offerings*' were the cereal-offerings which always accompanied the flesh-offerings, and this is the explanation of *RV*. The rendering of *AV* is '*meat offering*', where the word *meat* is used in the sixteenth-seventeenth-century sense of 'food' generally. Before the exile this offering (*minchah*) was a gift-offering; the word means 'tribute', and the offering was brought on the principle that a man must never come before a king without a gift. The word used for '*peace offerings*' is descriptive of one aspect of the ordinary flesh-offering, which was largely eaten by the worshippers. There is much dispute as to its significance, and perhaps the rite signified many things. Some say that this sacred meal was a shared meal between God and His people, a rite by which the communion between them was kept alive and strengthened. Some say that it was a meal which gave the eater 'peace, health, life', both physical and spiritual. Others say that the animal was sanctified by the priest so that it was regarded as being 'god', even to the extent that the worshipper could eat of this holy food and have the life of God strengthened in himself. Many of these ideas are to be found in teachings concerning the Lord's Supper, or Holy Communion.

5²⁵. The natural answer to the question is 'No'. Few verses have occasioned more difference of opinion, and often the opinion is decided by considerations of modern liturgical practice. It seems plain that both Amos (here) and Jeremiah (7^{22}) were of the opinion that there were no sacrifices in the desert in the old days before the entry into Canaan, those glorious days when all was well. They were certainly right to the extent that the ritual of the Hebrews in Solomon's temple was unknown before the entry into Canaan. When the Hebrews entered Canaan, they took over the Canaanite language, Canaanite ways of life, Canaanite religious rites, and sometimes even the Canaanite gods and goddesses. The Rechabites fought hard against it all. The prophets sought always to purge the rites of all idolatrous and immoral associations, and in general they did not like the sacrificial cult. Probably in the desert, there were firstling-offerings of beasts made on extempore altars of stone, and there may have been regular religious rites at certain times of the months and the years. Certain it is that the prophets were violently against the religious rites of their time; not thus should God be worshipped. If the worship and the sacrificial system were to be retained, then the people must '*rend their heart and not their garments*' (cf. Joel 2^{13}; see also Ps 51^{16-17}).

5^{26}. Read *RV*m '*ye shall take up* (i.e. carry) . . .'. The name of the god is Sakkut, the Assyrian Sakkut-Nidib, whose star was Chewan, the Babylonian name for Saturn. Each Babylonian deity was associated with one of the planets or first magnitude stars. The Jewish scribes deliberately changed the vowels of these names, and put in the vowels of the word *shiqquts* (detested thing), an abominable word for an abominable thing. Sometimes they changed the vowels of the hated idolatrous word to the vowels of the word *bosheth* (shameful thing), another horrid word for a horrid thing—e.g. Molech (for Melech), Tophet (for Tephet), Ashtoreth (for Astarte). Sometimes they even substituted the word Bosheth itself for Baal—e.g. Ishbosheth for Ishbaal (2 Sam 2^8 and 1 Chr 8^{33}).

6^{1-7}: Woe to the rich

The chief men of Samaria live in luxury and think they rule the best and most favoured of all countries; they are indifferent to Israel's serious malady. When disaster comes, they will be the first to be deported.

6¹. '*that are at ease in Zion, and to them*'. Probably a later insertion to direct the prophecy against the southern kingdom of Judah also.

'*To whom the house of Israel* [shall] *come*'. The addition of 'shall' is demanded by the Hebrew; thus the words are a threat of exile, being a relative clause dependent on '*the nations*'.

6². '*Calneh*', '*Hamath the great*', and '*Gath*'. If these cities are regarded as being already destroyed, then the passage is later than 711 B.C., when both Gath and Kulunu (the Calno of Isa 10⁹) were destroyed. But Amos may simply be comparing Samaria with greater cities, to try to convince her that she is not as wonderful and secure as she thinks. The last half of verse 2 should read 'are you better than these kingdoms? or is your border greater than theirs?'

6³ᵇ. Read 'but have brought close the enthronement of violence'.

6⁷ᵇ. Read 'and the shouting of the sprawlers shall depart'.

The paragraph shows the folly of saying with the Preacher: '*a man hath no better thing under the sun, than to eat, and to drink, and to be merry*' (Ecc 8¹⁵; see Lk 12¹⁹). A man does not need to be a millionaire in order to be satisfied with enjoying himself, taking no thought for anything else. The history of nations shows that when men and women put personal enjoyment and satisfaction first, they are piling up trouble for the future. The great example of antiquity is the Rome of the Emperors, with its banquets and weeks-ends at Pompeii and Baii for the rich, and circuses for the poor. The modern commercialization of entertainment in all its forms must fill any student of history with the greatest apprehension. But these things are only the symptoms of a deep-seated disease. The disease is that men have ceased to have any ultimate purpose in their lives. They have no aim in life except to live in the immediate present. They have no vision of the future, and '*Where there is no vision, the people cast off all restraint*' (Prov 29¹⁸), or (*AV*) '*the people perish*'. One attempt at a cure is to warn men of the deadly peril of the road they are travelling, but this approach usually fails. Men will not listen to tales of woe in times of apparent personal prosperity. The fact is that men must get back once more a sense of ultimate values; they must believe that there is something more than today and the immediate satisfaction of desires. They must learn again that this something matters much more than anything they can see. Some see this 'ultimate value' in culture and knowledge, and many men find a purpose and meaning in life along these lines. The Christian knows that the real cure is a religious one, and that men must be brought back to a vital and living faith in God. The parable of the pearl of great price (Mt 13⁴⁵⁻⁶) is apposite here. It is foolish to deny that cultural interests such as art, music and literature are valuable; it is foolish to discount any form of knowledge. These human things are good; but the pearl of great price is best.

Much of the modern lack of 'vision' is due to the denial of absolute categories,[1] to the idea that there are no values except those a man makes for himself, and that there is no absolute good, but only what is good to each man. This may be true in the aesthetic world, for the estimation of beauty is largely subjective. But the man who denies any truth apart from what he sees to be truth, ends by having nothing apart from himself, and that only in the immediate present.

Again, it is easy for Christians to content themselves with a negative attitude to types of conduct of which they do not approve. One result of this is that Christians are sometimes represented, with a certain amount of justification, as objectors, kill-joys, men who are always trying to stop other people doing the things they themselves do not want to do. We need to remember that our major argument about conduct is always a Christian one. Thus our ultimate test of morals is Christian: does this action of mine cause my brother to stumble, my brother for whom Christ died? Similarly, the argument for the Christian use of Sunday is a Christian argument. Why should a non-Christian behave himself on any particular day as a Christian? What is wrong is that the root of his conduct is non-Christian, and this is the aspect to which we must chiefly direct our attention; no other argument is of much avail. Make him a Christian and then we shall not need to argue with him.

The eighth century B.C. was a time of great prosperity for the upper class and for the new merchant class which had grown up as a result of the enlightened trade policy of Omri and

---

[1] See H. G. Wells, *First and Last Things*.

Ahab. Both Hebrew kingdoms, Israel and Judah, were fortunate in that at this time they both had efficient kings, Jeroboam II in the North and Azariah (Uzziah) in the South. At the beginning of the century an Assyrian king had destroyed Damascus (see p. 11) and thus removed the only serious nearby rival of the two Hebrew kingdoms. Egypt was weak, and so also was Assyria herself for the first half of the century. In this way the two kingdoms, and particularly Israel which was always economically stronger than Judah, were able to control the caravan routes and grow rich. The danger of prosperity is greater than that of poverty. It is said that at the height of their prosperity the Spartans sent to the oracle at Delphi to ask whether anything could harm them. The answer was: 'Yes; prosperity.'

6^{8-11}: Pride and its penalty

Verses 9-10 are a prose interpolation inserted into an oracle (verses 8 and 11) which says that God is going to abandon the proud capital and everything in it: '*the great house*' (6^{11}) will be smashed into fragments and '*the small house*' cleft into fissures.

6^8. For '*excellency*', read 'pride' (*RV*m). The Greek Version has *hubris*, the insolence of a man who thinks himself equal to God. According to ancient ideas this was man's greatest sin. This is the Hebrew moral of Genesis 11^4; the ancient city of Babylon (Babylon is the Greek spelling, Babel the Hebrew, Babilu—gate of god—the Babylonian) seemed impious to the early Hebrew nomad who knew nothing higher than his own tent poles, because the great towering temple (*ziggurat*) seemed to reach up to heaven. The crime of a much later king of Babylon was that he said in his heart: '*I will ascend into heaven, I will exalt my throne above the stars of God, . . . I will be like the Most High*' (Isa 14^{13-14}. See 2 Chr 26^{16}; Isa 2^{11}; Lk 1^{21}; Jas 4^6; 1 Pet 5^5, and elsewhere). The modern Hebrew word for this kind of pride is *chutspah*.[2] The Greeks called it *hubris*. Aeschylus's play *The Persae* is built on the folly of *hubris*: the immediate cause of the destruction of the Persian fleet at Salamis in 480 B.C. was the skill of Themistocles and the valour of the Athenians fighting for their

[2] See Miss Naomi Jacob's *That Wild Lie* . . .

liberty, but the ultimate cause was that the Persian king had sought to abrogate to himself divine functions. The Hebrews said that pride was the sin of Adam; he sought to be '*as God*' (Gen 3⁵). Man is made always to be reaching upward, and it is this quality which has made him what he is; but God is God and man is man, and never the twain shall meet except in Christ. God requires of man that he shall fulfil His justice, be faithful to the covenant, and *walk humbly* with Him. See note on Micah 6⁸. All is of grace.

6¹⁰. In this dreadful epidemic, a man's uncle and the undertaker will carry out his corpse and call to see if there is any other body there. Things are so bad, that not even the Name of God may be invoked.

6¹²: No sense

The difficulty of the Hebrew is shown by the fact that the English Versions have to insert '*there*' in an attempt to give an adequate translation. It is best to split the Hebrew words differently so as to read: 'Can horses gallop up a crag, or does one plough the sea with oxen?'

Nobody who has any sense will expect either the one thing or the other. The situation in the law courts is just as silly. The kind of justice that is dispensed there makes the whole system nonsense.

6¹³⁻¹⁴: A false dawn

Jeroboam II captured these two places from Syria (Damascus). The people who hail these successes as the prelude to greater things are foolish; Israel will be harassed from one end of the country to the other.

7¹⁻⁹: Three chances

Amos sees three visions of judgement: locusts, fire, and plumbline. He pleads twice for forgiveness, and God relents; but not the third time.

7¹. '*latter growth*'. The crop of grass which grows after the latter rain, i.e. the spring growth.

'*The king's mowings*'. This supposes that the king took the whole of the first crop, the best and sweetest grass of all; but the more natural translation is 'the king's shearings', thus making the end of the verse an explanatory gloss explaining the time of the year. The locust swarm is threatening to destroy the spring crop of grass.

7²: It is best to read 'and as was it making an end of eating . . .'. The meaning now is that God prevents the locusts from making an absolutely clean sweep of the crop.

When it is said that '*the LORD repented*' (7³, ⁶), the meaning is that God changed His mind. 'Repent' is a mistranslation, due to a lack of understanding of the proper meaning of the Hebrew word. The word strictly means 'breathe pantingly' (cf. of a horse); there may be a sense of sorrow sometimes when the word is used, but this is by no means necessary. One form of the verb is usually translated 'comfort'. Here again it is easy to be misled, because the word does not mean 'comfort in the midst of sorrow', but rather 'comfort *out of* sorrow', ensure an end of all weeping, dry the tears and bring permanent consolation. This is because here also the meaning of the word has to do with 'change the mind and attitude', 'turn round and be different'. The regular Greek equivalent in the Old Testament is also used of the Holy Spirit in the New Testament. When, therefore, we speak of the Holy Spirit the Comforter, we need to remember that here also the idea is of a Person who causes men to change their minds, causes them to be different. The word means Convincer to a far greater extent than Comforter. If we do indeed use the word 'Comforter' of the Holy Spirit, we need to remember that it is essentially effective comfort, an end of fear and sorrow and tears. But the word refers to changing out of sin, turning men round so that their faces are set toward heaven.

7⁴. '*to contend with fire*'. The *RSV* is better, '*for a judgement by fire*', but it is probably best to read 'a flaming fire'. The Hebrew is uncertain, and the ancient versions all guess.

'*the land*': note the *RV*m '*the portion*'. The Hebrew word used is that which describes one man's share of the common land outside the village, his Strip, as in medieval England. The Lord's 'Portion' is Israel (cf. Deut 32⁹: 'the Lord's portion is his people', where the same word is used).

The plumb-line is the test of uprightness and truth. This is the test which God will apply to Israel. It is the test which is applied in the course of history to every people and nation (see Mt 26[52]). Men reap what they sow (Mt 7[16], Lk 6[44]). Such is the justice of this world.

7[10-17]: Amos at Bethel

Jeroboam's own dynasty had been established by the prophets preaching sedition against the House of Omri and of his son Ahab. The priest of Bethel tells Amos to go home and earn his bread by prophesying there. Amos indignantly denies that he is a professional prophet, and finally speaks of the dreadful fate which awaits Amaziah's family and the whole nation.

(Dr G. R. Driver has recently argued that Amos does not deny that he was a prophet. He would translate: 'Am not I a prophet? God called me from following the flock.')

7[14]. '*a prophet's son*'. This does not mean a man whose actual father was a prophet, but 'a member of the prophetic guild'. The phrase 'son of' is a Hebrew idiom; e.g. 'son of man' is an alternative way of saying 'man', member of the group called 'mankind'. In pre-exilic times there were groups of prophets attached to shrines, and they sometimes went in procession from place to place uttering strange ecstatic cries and whirling in strange dances (1 Sam 10[10]).

7[14]. The 'sycomore' belongs to the fig family, and produces a small fig-like fruit, commonly eaten by the poor. Some say that this fruit has to be nipped or pierced to release parasites with which it is infested, and that then it is fit for food; but this is not certain, and it is best to follow *RV* with the indefinite 'dresser'. The 'sycamine' tree is a mulberry and is therefore quite distinct from the sycomore. Our sycamore is a maple and is different from both.

Amos was conscious of a definite call. God called him and '*took* [him] *from after the sheep*'; he was a shepherd. Shepherds played a large part in Hebrew history. The patriarchs were shepherds. David was a shepherd, the first of the royal line which lasted for over four centuries, the type of King Messiah, the sweet singer of Israel. Here is Amos the shepherd, the first of the writing prophets, those men whose contribution to the religion of Israel is so marked and decisive. Moses was keeping sheep when God called him at the Bush. Kings are often called shepherds, and the figure of feeding the sheep is used for the functions of a king (2 Sam 5², 7⁷). God is Israel's shepherd (Ps 80¹) and He is 'my shepherd' (Ps 23¹) too. Shepherds straight from their flocks were the first to greet the Christ-child. Jesus called Himself 'the good shepherd' (Jn 10¹⁴), and the good shepherd *'layeth down his life for the sheep'* (Gen 31⁴⁰, 1 Sam 17³⁴⁻⁶, Amos 3¹²). The sheep are helpless without their shepherd, scattered, and easy prey for the marauding animal (Num 27¹⁷, 1 Kings 22¹⁷, Ezek 34⁵). The shepherd stands for protection, the utmost loving care, and in the last resort self-sacrifice. The Prophet of the Exile pictures God as a shepherd leading back home to Jerusalem exiled Israel (Isa 40¹¹), leading them on from oasis to oasis, carrying the lambs in his arms, and caring specially for the ewes that are heavy with young. (The Hebrew word in Isaiah 40¹¹ properly means 'give suck whilst pregnant'; *RV* takes the word one way and *AV* the other, but both are correct.) In the first years of the sorely persecuted Christian Church, Hermas saw visions of Christ the Shepherd coming to the rescue of His flock. The book which records these visions, *The Shepherd of Hermas*, was held in great esteem and was very nearly accepted as Scripture.

Amos was conscious of a call to be a prophet which overrode everything else. This imperious call is a necessity for the preacher. The man who is called must leave everything and follow (1 Kings 19¹⁹⁻²¹, Mk 1¹⁶⁻²⁰, 2¹⁴). In the Gospels, 'called' often means 'invited' (Mt 22¹⁴); but in the writings of Paul, and also in the Gospel according to John (15¹⁶, ¹⁹), the word means 'effectively called, chosen'. When we say that a man is called of God, this is what we mean. All men are called of God in the sense that 'the invitation is to all' (*MHB* 323), but not all are called effectively. The relation between the free choice on the part of a man and the divine compulsion of which some are conscious is a matter of continual debate. Perhaps the best solution is to regard the matter as a statement concerning religious experience. When a man first becomes a follower of Christ, he is conscious that it is his own choice. He says that he chooses Christ, and this is true; the preacher 'offers Christ', and the man either accepts or rejects Him. But the longer a man has been in the Way, the more he has grown into full Christian manhood, the less he talks of himself choosing Christ and the more he talks in terms of Christ choosing him. He knows that the very first stirrings in his heart were the work of the Holy Spirit. The idea of its being man's choice belongs to the experience of Justification; the idea of its being God's choice belongs to the experience of Sanctification. Both ideas are true, but they belong to different stages of Christian experience. As soon as the one description is used of the other phase, the statement is wrong.

The prophet is not a man who foretells the future at a far distance, though he may do this on occasion. All Old Testament prophets speak of times immediately ahead; long-term prophecy is not their natural function. The prophet speaks forth the word of God, but since it is the Word of God that he speaks, we find him speaking a greater truth than he knows. He speaks to the men of his own time concerning the events of his own time, but he also speaks that Word of God which is true for all time. It is our task to separate the application to the prophet's own time from the truth which abides for all time, and then, prayerfully, to seek the application to our own time. The Bible student who reads his Bible only to find in it prophecies relating to days far ahead of the time of the prophet is woefully neglecting the real function of the prophet. Most of the words of a prophet are concerned with the nature and work of the Saviour God, whose thought and ways to man he attempts to set forth to his own generation, leading men to Him, and urging them to turn to Him. The prophet is primarily an evangelist, a preacher of the Gospel of the living Saviour God.

7^{16}. '*drop not*' is the literal translation of the Hebrew word. It is used of clouds dripping water, of hands dripping with myrrh, and of words falling from a man's lips. It is used in Job 29^{22} of ordinary speech, and occasionally, as here, of the words of a prophet.

7^{17}. '*A land that is unclean*' is any land that is not the holy-clean soil of Israel; it is a foreign land. The prophet is threatening exile for the northern kingdom of Israel.

8^{1-3}: The end has come

The prophet is saying that the disaster is close at hand and will come suddenly. Israel is ripe for punishment.

8¹. '*summer fruit*'. The reference is really to the very great heat of the late summer.

8². '*The end*'. Amos is here making a pun—'summer' is *qayits*; 'end' is *qayts*. In tropical and semi-tropical climates the illustration of ripe fruit in high summer can be appreciated much better than here in Britain. Ripe fruit quickly deteriorates, and is '*as the hasty fruit before the summer; which when he that looketh upon it seeth, while it is yet in his hand he eateth it up*' (Isa 28⁴, *AV*).

8³. '*the songs of the temple*'. Follow the Greek Version (Septuagint) and read: 'and the singing women of the palace (*RV*m) shall howl in that day.' The last four words of this verse are difficult, and it is best to omit '*with silence*' as wholly uncertain.

8⁴⁻⁸: Wealthy rogues

Amos again charges the wealthy merchants with harsh treatment of the poor. Here the charges are not of sharp practice within the law, but of definite cheating—the use of false measures and the selling of the sweepings of wheat as good grain.

8⁵. The new-month-day and the sabbath were the two monthly holidays of pre-exilic times. After the Exile the sabbath became a weekly festival and took on the sombre hue of a taboo day.

'*making the ephah small*' is 'giving short measure'. The ephah was roughly equal to the modern bushel.

'*and the shekel great*'. The custom was to weigh the amount of gold required in any purchase; Amos charges them with using heavier weights than were correct in order to get more money, and also with using untrue scales.

8⁸. The Hebrew has 'it shall rise like the light', but all are agreed that the letter *yodh* (the smallest letter of the alphabet) has been omitted, and we should read 'rise like the Nile'.

8⁹⁻¹⁰: Darkness and sorrow

The prophet's words continue to be full of disaster. He can see no slightest hope for unrepentant Israel.

8¹⁰. 'feasts'. The reference is to the joyful pilgrimages, especially to the Feast of Ingathering in the autumn, part of which became the Feast of Tabernacles in the post-exilic period.

'*sackcloth upon all loins and baldness upon every head*' are the two ancient mourning customs of Palestine. The custom of shaving part of the head was forbidden in Deuteronomy 14¹, but in the time of Amos the custom was regarded as being proper. It became officially illegal in the vigorous attempt in Josiah's time, a hundred or so years later, to get rid of every vestige of ancient Canaanite custom. The life-giving hair was given to the dead that they might find some kind of life beyond the grave. See note on Micah 1¹⁶.

8¹¹⁻¹²: The most deadly famine of all

This is a famine of the Word of God, worse than lack of food and drink. They will stagger from one end of the land to the other, and still go hungry.

The references to '*the word of the LORD*' could provide a text for a sermon on food for life eternal, but better passages for this purpose are to be found in John 6, where the feeding of the five thousand is allegorized, or in John 4¹⁰⁻¹⁴. See also 1 Corinthians 10⁴, where Paul makes use of the Rabbinic tradition that the Rock of Rephidim (Ex 16⁶) followed the Israelites to the borders of Canaan, giving them heavenly water as well as the manna.

8¹³⁻¹⁴: Even the Young and Strong shall Fall

The punishment of idolators is certain and final.

8¹⁴. '*the sin of Samaria*'. Probably this should be 'Ashimah of Samaria'. This goddess was worshipped by Jews in Egypt in the fifth century B.C. as the secondary wife of Yahweh, Anath (Queen of Heaven) being the chief wife. She is mentioned also in 2 Kings 17³⁰. Whether this goddess was actually introduced by the settlers or not, it is certain that the queen of heaven was worshipped more or less continuously through the years (Jer 44¹⁸⁻¹⁹). Modern archaeological discoveries have shown that every word spoken by the prophets concerning Israel's continued and persistent apostasy is true.

'*the way*'. Many here would read 'thy Darling', making it another reference to a heathen god.

9¹⁻⁴: Especially the shrine

The punishment will begin with the shrine, presumably Bethel the royal sanctuary, because that is the centre and core of Israel's sin. There will be no escape, wherever they may flee; God will search them out and destroy them.

9¹. '*chapiters*', 'capitals of the pillars'. For '*on the head of all of them*' read the more intelligible 'with the sum total of them all'.

9². 'hell', Sheol, the place of the dead. But here the reference is topographical; Amos means 'though they dig deep, God will still find them'.

9³. The reference is to the dense vegetation which in those days covered the whole ridge.

'*the serpent*'. The reference is to the Monster of the ancient Creation Myth, who was defeated and fastened in the depths of the sea. When the sea roars, it is the serpent trying to get free (Ps 93³). In Revelation 12⁹, 13¹ the serpent becomes the Anti-Christ. The Hebrews identified every enemy of God with this Monster—Babylon, Egypt, and at last the Beast of the Apocalypse.

False worship merits and receives condemnation. The fact that a place is regarded as holy does not save it in the time of judgement. Holiness means belonging to God. A holy man is a man who belongs to God. A holy building is a building that belongs to God. But if the man who belongs to God ceases to do the things of God, he ceases to be holy. If a Church turns away from the way of Christ, that Church ceases to be holy. Her doctrine must be pure; her ministers must be true followers of Christ; her people must be lovers of God. For buildings, the continued devotion and worship of holy people is necessary. For people, continued faith and repentance is necessary. Holiness is not a thing in itself; it is a relationship between persons, between God on the one side and man on the other. A place can be holy only when this relationship between God and man is maintained in association with it. Holy ground is the ground where man meets with God in humility and faith. Where there is no true worship, there is no holy place, and in the judgement that place must be brought down.

9⁵⁻⁶: The palace in the skies

The first part of this oracle is practically a repetition of 8⁸. The second part pictures the terraces of the heavenly temple, fixed on an arched dome and towering up into the sky.

9⁷⁻⁸ᵃ: The rejection of Israel

This oracle marks the end of the genuine prophecies of Amos. It speaks of the utter rejection of Israel. The rescue of Israel from Egypt means no more than any other movement of the peoples.

9⁷. The Ethiopians are named because they were a distant people of whom the Israelites would have heard. There is, of course, no slightest suggestion that the colour of their skin is the point at issue; there is no warrant anywhere in the Bible for that kind of idea. '*Kaphtor*' is Crete, the Philistines being the last survivors of the ancient Minoan civilization. '*Kir*' is unknown, but it was away east of Damascus.

9⁸. The oracle ends with '*earth*'. To be chosen by God does not mean to be chosen for ever. The chosen people that does not choose to walk in His ways ceases to be a chosen people. Israel has turned away from God, and in so doing has lost that special favour which ensured her continued existence. The rescue from Egypt was the mightiest of the Acts of God, because the choice of Israel was involved in it. The prophets were always referring to it. It marked their beginning as a nation; it was firm evidence of God's visitation in saving power. But now that Israel has turned away from God, the rescue from Egypt has no religious significance. It has merely the same historical significance as the movement of the Philistines from Crete or of the Syrians from far away Kir. It was just a

D

migration of a people, the sort of thing that happens in this world when nations grow restless or need more room. It has no special meaning.

History is the recounting of events woven into a pattern. The historian decides what is the pattern and writes his history accordingly. John Richard Green writes his history of England as the story of the growth of a people. Some historians of the United States of America adopt the theme 'Go west, young man' and make the story of the United States a story of the pioneer, first out to the west and then into all the world; others tell it as the story of the struggle of the central government against the big financial trusts. But always history must have a theme. If the historian says that he sees no pattern, no thread running through the story, then he is making that absence of pattern and thread his theme. When the Bible writers wrote their history, their theme was the work of the mighty Saviour God manifested in the story of His people Israel. This is what the Bible is about, first in the Old Testament, and then in the New Testament, where the people Israel is the fellowship of those who accept Christ as Saviour and God. Amos here is giving up the theme. He says the story is over now. It no longer has any meaning. What once was the high point of a nation's experience has now ceased to have any meaning at all. There is no longer a people of God named Israel. There is no such history.

9^{8b–9}: The new Israel

Here we have the words of a later writer who cannot leave the matter where Amos leaves it. He says that Judah, the southern kingdom, will not be swept away. Judah is now Israel, the people of God. Israel will wander to and fro, and will continue to wander. The reference to 'not a grain falling to the earth' can easily be misunderstood. Our first impression is that not a grain will be lost. But that is not the meaning: it is rather that not a grain will be exempted from the continual shaking to and fro.

9¹⁰: Death to the sinners

This is a difficult verse. The easiest explanation is that it is an addition by a scribe who took the end of the previous verse to mean that all Judah would be saved from the Exile which began in 597 B.C. He says that the sinners will not be saved, but only the faithful righteous.

9¹¹⁻¹⁵: Happy endings

Verses 11 and 12 must belong to days after the Exile, when Judah had fallen and there were no longer any kings of David's line in Jerusalem. This was the time when Edom sought to enrich herself at the expense of unfortunate Judah. Verse 13 speaks of such bounty and prosperity that the reapers will not have finished their harvest before it is time for the ploughmen to begin. The last two verses are the happy ending which seems to be demanded in all the prophetic books.

9¹⁴. *'bring again the captivity'*. Read 'change the fortune'; cf. Job 42¹⁰. And so we come to the end of Amos. Please God there shall be a 'happy ending' in the presence of God.

Hosea

HOSEA was a Northerner, but there is no evidence as to the actual place of his birth. It has been suggested that he was a baker by trade, but this is a guess based on his reference in chapter seven to baking. It is generally agreed that his wife Gomer-bath-Diblaim was unfaithful to him, and that at least two of the children she bore were not Hosea's children. Some say she was a harlot before he married her, and others that she became one after marriage. In any case, Hosea's persistent love for his erring wife taught him something of God's persistent love for erring Israel.

Hosea's great contribution to Hebrew religion is this idea of 'steadfast love', God's persistent love for the people whom He chose and with whom He made the Covenant. It is this steadfast love which is the basis of the Christian 'grace'.

Hosea, like Amos, prophesied during the reign of Jeroboam II (788-747 B.C.), but it is generally maintained that it was right at the end of the reign. Most scholars would thus make Hosea's activity some fifteen years or so later than that of Amos, and thus fifteen years nearer the destruction of the northern kingdom of Israel. We have the same background of wickedness and immoral worship; but whereas Amos is primarily concerned with matters of conduct, Hosea is concerned with Israel's relationship with Yahweh. It is as though Amos thought in terms of doing God's will, but Hosea thought in terms of loyalty and love to God.

Most of the book is from the prophet Hosea, though there are sections here and there which seem to be from later times. The text of the Hebrew is often corrupt, and there are some instances where it is quite impossible to say what is really meant. This is probably the only Northern collection of oracles, and it is only by a miracle that it has survived.

1¹: Introduction

This is the usual editorial note fixing the date of the prophet. The dates of the Hebrew kings are uncertain, but Uzziah's

reign may have ended as late as 744 B.C., and Jeroboam's
death may have been as late as 746 B.C.

1²⁻⁹: Gomer and her children

Hosea married Gomer-bath-Diblaim. At first all went well,
but after the birth of the first child, she went astray, and
although she bore two more children, they were not by Hosea.
Hosea gave all three children symbolic names. He thus made
their births significant for the fate of Israel.

1². The Hebrew is a little curious. The Rabbis held that the
verse means that the first time God spoke through a prophet,
it was through Hosea. That is why Hosea is placed as the
first of the Twelve Prophets.

'*a wife of whoredoms*'. Some think this means that she was a
harlot before Hosea married her. But **1³** says '*and bare him a
son*', whereas **1⁶** and **1⁸** have '*bare*' but not '*him*'. Also, if the
allegory is to be complete, we need a Gomer who is at first
faithful and later becomes unfaithful, just as Israel was
faithful at first to Yahweh and later was false to Him.

1⁴. '*Jezreel*'. The reference is to the river of blood through
which Jehu waded to the throne. Hosea says that the Jehu
dynasty, and with it the kingdom of Israel, must pay the full
price of the blood-guilt, even though Jehu had wiped out all
the male line of the dynasty of Omri.

1⁷ is a later insertion to say that Judah will be saved even
though Israel will be destroyed.

There was a time when names were significant, and descriptive of the person who bore them. In this country men used
to be called John the Wheelwright and Tom o' the Hill. Now,
it is for the most part only by-names (nick-names) which are
descriptive. Some Bible names are well suited to the character
and life of the person concerned. The name Elijah means 'Jah
(Yahweh) is my God.' Jeremiah probably means 'Yah hurls',
which is a good description of a diffident prophet who was
always being projected into situations for which he was not
naturally apt, but was always given grace sufficient for the
task and was enabled to find strength even out of his bitter

experience: he was the friendly man who was doomed to be largely without friends and thereby found a fellowship with God as none had done before him; he was the patriot who was called to prophesy disaster to his country and to advise abject surrender to the foreigner, because he knew that 'patriotism is not enough'. Barnabas is the 'son of exhortation', the man who went about looking for the best in people: he saw good in Saul of Tarsus when nobody else saw it, and he held on to John Mark when Paul would have abandoned him; he was thus responsible for the first of the gospel writers, and it was he who brought Paul into the work, not only by acting as his sponsor in Jerusalem at the beginning, but also by bringing him back to Antioch in Syria, that first great centre of missionary work. But sometimes, as here, the names are 'signs and portents' (Isa 8¹⁸); that is, the giving of the name ensures the fulfilment of the Word and Purpose of God which the name embodies. When Isaiah gives his two sons their strange names (Isa 8³, 7³), he ensures that what the names say will come to pass. See also Isaiah 7¹², where King Ahaz does everything he can to prevent Isaiah giving him a sign, because he knows that if the sign is given, the rest will then surely follow; but Isaiah insists on giving the sign whatever Ahaz may say. The same inevitability is involved in the sign of the child which the young woman is to bear (Isa 7¹⁴; see also Mt 1²¹, *RV*). This use of names as signs is due to the strong conviction that God will never leave alone this world which He has made; He is always active in it to seek and to save that which is lost.

Hosea's comment on Jehu's wholesale slaughter of the males of Ahab's family is a significant reversal of the attitude of 2 Kings 9-10, where the wholesale slaughter is regarded on the whole as being meritorious. '*All they that take the sword shall perish with the sword*' (Mt 26⁵²). It is probable that Jehu was able to save the North for Yahweh only by the complete extirpation of the pro-Baal House of Ahab, and perhaps rough times demanded rough ways. Nevertheless, it remains true that murder breeds murder and war breeds war. The only way to avoid the ceaseless chain of strife is by absorbing the injury or the insult, and by not retaliating. This is the soft answer that turns away wrath, the presenting of the other cheek, the going the second mile. The dynasty of Jehu did eventually pay the penalty for the slaughter through which it originally became established, and the Kingdom of Israel followed soon after—not immediately, as 1^4 may intend, but after twenty-five troubled and stormy years.

The interpolated verse (1^7) is important. There are several ways in which Hosea is a forerunner of Jesus, the succession being through Jeremiah. Here is the first stage in a continued revelation which reaches its climax in John 18^{36}: '*My kingdom is not of this world . . .*' (see Zech 4^6). At first, salvation is thought of in terms of national success by force of arms, and many still think in this fashion. But beginning from Hosea, there has always been an element in Jewry which has thought of Israel's greatness as being different from that of the nations, though this tradition has been largely overshadowed in recent times by a militant Zionism. The prophet Hosea realizes that Judah's greatness will not be gained by military prowess, but God will save her people in His own way.

1^{10}–2^1: The restored kingdom

Some think that these verses should follow 3^5, and both these and others think that they are later than Hosea. The verses envisage a restored united kingdom with a tremendous increase in the population of the North. The phrase '*shall go up from the land*' (1^{11}) may refer to both Israel and Judah coming up from the country to Jerusalem for the great feasts, but some think it may refer to the dispersed of both north and south coming back to the homeland. It is impossible to speak with any certainty of the date and precise meaning of the section. But it certainly involves a reversal of the judgement of the previous verses, because '*the day of Jezreel*' is now to be a great and glorious day, and the negative of the names of the two daughters is itself to be negatived.

There are many references in the Old Testament to God repenting. The clearest reference is Numbers 23^{19}, in one of the Balaam oracles. The translation '*repent*' is not good. The word really means 'change the mind' (see note in Amos 7^1). In the Balaam oracle, the meaning is that God will not change His mind and say anything different from what He said before when He spoke good things concerning Israel. God is said to change His mind concerning both the good fortune that He intended and the evil fortune that He intended. Both occur in Jeremiah $18^{8, 10}$. The change from good to evil involves the penalty and wages of sin. The change from evil to good depends upon repentance on the part of man. God does not change His mind in any irresponsible fashion, but humanly speaking He is always in a dilemma because of man's sin. The wages of sin is death, but '*I have no pleasure in the death of him that dieth, saith the LORD God; wherefore turn yourselves, and live*' (Ezek 18³²). And so, in the prophets, we get this continual alternation, and nowhere more regularly than in Hosea. God is always offering life and salvation to the sinner. The name Jezreel, which was once a word of death, can become a word of life. The very place of Israel's rejection (1¹⁰) can become the place of Israel's renewed acceptance.

2²⁻²³: The punishment and restoration of wayward Israel

The prophet longs to have his wife back again, and bids the children plead with her. Perhaps after all she will find that she was better off at home, and will return. Similarly, God longs for Israel to return to Him. He will entice Israel back again into the desert where all went well, and will begin the courtship all over again.

2⁵. The '*lovers*' are the baals, local manifestations of the great god Baal, the Rider of the Clouds, the rain-god of Canaan, and so the fertility god.

2¹². '*forest*', the bad-lands (cf. 2 Sam 18⁸ and the note on Amos 3⁴).

2¹³. '*the days of the Baalim*'. The feast-days on which Israel worshipped the baals, but especially the first day of the great Autumn Harvest Feast (Ingathering), which was the special day of thanksgiving and the New Year's Day when the fate of the incoming year was decided (see note on Amos 5¹⁸⁻²⁰).

'*burned incense*'. In pre-exilic passages this phrase should be translated 'burned sacrifice'. The word strictly means 'burn up in smoke'. Incense was introduced after the exile and was due to Babylonian influence.

2¹⁴. '*speak comfortably*' is literally 'speak to the heart', '*speak tenderly*' (*RSV*), but it often means 'make love to'.

2¹⁵. '*the valley of Achor*' (Josh 7²⁶) was the valley through which Israel first entered the Promised Land under Joshua. When Israel enters again into Canaan this Valley of Trouble will be a door of hope.

'*make answer*', i.e. respond to the overtures of her lover.

2¹⁶. '*Ishi*' is the ordinary Hebrew for 'my man'. '*Baali*' means my husband (master, lord)'.

2²¹. '*answer*', i.e. 'respond to the call of', as in the Adult School translation.

Who is it really that gives Israel the corn and wine and oil? Is it Baal, the Canaanite god, the ancient fertility god of the land, the god whom Israel found there when she entered? Or is it Yahweh, the God who brought Israel out of Egypt, through the desert, and entered Canaan with her? Hosea complains that the Israelites have fallen in with Canaanite custom in ascribing the fertility to Baal. They do not realize that they owe this also to Yahweh. This is the point at issue in 1 Kings 18. Elijah bids the people make up their minds and decide which God they are really going to worship, Baal or Yahweh. It is all a question of rain. Who withheld the rains for three years? Who can give rain forthwith? It is the Yahweh offering that is burned up, and immediately the prophet and his young man go to the top of Carmel to look out over the sea for the rain-cloud to come. Quickly it sweeps in over the parched land in a tremendous deluge, and Ahab has to urge his horses to their utmost speed in order to get home before Esdraelon becomes an impossible quagmire, as it once did to Sisera's undoing. Beyond doubt, when Israel entered Canaan, she took over everything Canaanite—language, custom, and even religion. The prophets had to fight hard to maintain anything like pure worship for Yahweh, and every word they say concerning Israel's waywardness, vacillation and apostasy is true.

2⁶. '*I will hedge up thy way with thorns*'. God has more ways than one of seeking to bring sinners to repentance. There is the undying appeal of Christ's dying love, and by the power of the Holy Spirit this can bring men back to Him. But there is another method in that '*the way of transgressors is hard*' (Prov 13¹⁵, *AV*). This may work through conscience if they are not altogether hardened in sin, or it may work through the progressive difficulties raised up by progressive wrong-doing. Israel will find it increasingly difficult to continue in her wayward path. Her own actions will increase her distress, until she gives up and elects to try once more the ways of her true God. When she loses everything, she will find that Baal cannot provide her with the happiness or even with the bare sustenance she must have.

Hosea wants to go back again. He cannot turn back the pages of history, but he longs for the old courtship days to be repeated. To the prophets generally, the days before the entry into Canaan were Israel's happy days. If only Israel can be enticed back to the desert again, even if it means exile from Canaan, perhaps there can be a new start. The name of Baal will be cut right out of the vocabulary and '*baali*' will even cease to be the normal way in which a woman speaks to her husband. Every trace and every use of the hated word must go. In this way even the remotest temptation will be removed. The best way to avoid falling into temptation is to avoid every slightest suggestion of it. The man who stands least chance of falling into a pit is the man who deliberately keeps as far as he can from the edge of it.

2^{19-20}. The basis of the new betrothal is to be '*righteousness, judgement, lovingkindness, mercies, faithfulness* and knowledge of the Lord'. To follow righteousness means to conform to the pattern laid down by the will of God, to act in accordance with His nature and character (see note on Amos 2^7). Judgement refers to the will of God which has been declared, and which is known by past experience and teaching; it is always 'God's justice'. 'Lovingkindness' is Coverdale's translation of the word *chesed*. This word has an original meaning of steadfastness, reliability (cf. Isa 40^6: all the steadfastness of man is like the wild flowers, here today and gone tomorrow, in contrast with the firm reliability of the word of God), but it comes to be used for the proper attitude which each party to a covenant should maintain toward the other. The tragedy of so much of Israel's history is that her *chesed* (faithfulness to the covenant; '*goodness*' in 6^4 is not correct) was like the morning cloud and the morning dew which soon disappear. The result of this continued unreliability of Israel was that Yahweh's *chesed* had more and more to consist of forgiveness and the love that could not give Israel up (11^8). This is why both the ancient Greek Version (Septuagint) and the Vulgate usually translated the word by 'pity, mercy', and this is also at the root of Coverdale's beautiful word 'lovingkindness'; Sir George Adam Smith favoured the rendering 'leal love'; another rendering is to be found in *MHB* 62³: 'Thy sure love, Thy tender care.' The word is essentially connected with the Covenant. In the Old Testament this 'covenant love' is not for all and sundry, but only for the People of the Covenant, Israel. In this connexion the most important verse in the New Testament is Ephesians 2¹⁴: '*and brake down the middle wall of partition*'. That selective love is now available for all mankind. Christ, by His death, opened the flood gates so that the mighty pent-up torrent of God's love should sweep through all the world. At the back of all this is the idea also that Israel became the People of God, not because of anything in them, but all because of God's goodwill and pleasure (cf. Deut 9⁶, etc.). Out of this complex we get the New Testament doctrine of Grace, God's free gift to every man, flowing out to all like a mighty stream. This grace is not to be likened to a large lake covering everywhere to an equal depth, but to a torrent mightily rushing. It is true that God loves all, but He loves each separate one as though he were the only one. The word translated '*mercies*' is usually concerned with God's compassion for mortal man, his short life and hard lot (Ps 103¹³ᶠ), and not with the idea of forgiveness. The use of the word '*emunah* (faithfulness) in verse 20 is very important. It means 'reliability', the complement of 'trust, faith'. Indeed the Greek Version here has *pistis*, which is Paul's word for 'faith'. This idea of 'trust, recumbency' is not the normal Greek usage, which is 'belief', the acceptance of a statement as being true, and so forth (this is the way the word is used in Jas 2¹⁸). Paul's use of the word is dependent upon the Hebrew use; he means by it a firm reliance on One who can be relied on. In Galatians 3¹¹ the meaning is that the just man (the righteous, the man who is right with God) shall live through relying completely upon the God who is thoroughly reliable, who can be relied upon. See John Wesley's sermon on 'Justification by Faith'. Note that the Greek word for 'justification' is closely allied to the word translated 'just' and means not so much 'made righteous' or 'treated as righteous' in an ethical sense (though this is involved), as 'made right with God' in a personal sense.

The climax is to be found in '*thou shalt know the* LORD', Here the emphasis is on personal knowledge in experience rather than on intellectual apprehension (see the note on Amos 3²). It is important that the preacher should be able to give reasons for the faith that is in him, and that he should take pains to understand the coldly critical, intellectual, semi-agnostic approach of many people in these days; but his own knowledge of God must be more than this. It must be based on personal awareness and personal trust. In other words, theology counts, and the preacher must be aware of theological problems and of the various arguments (to sneer at theology is sheer folly and ignorance, and shows a lack of understanding of the fullness of the call to preach); but he must also be aware of the personal, experimental side of religion, which is the ultimately really important aspect.

'The sympathy of nature' is evident in 2²¹⁻². This doctrine was a favourite one among the Stoics, who represented the dominant school of philosophers in New Testament times; they believed in the harmony of nature and loved its beauty. Notice that in the Old Testament, apart from the Song of Solomon, there is no appreciation of the beauty of Nature as such. The passages where nature rejoices, where the trees clap their hands and the valleys laugh and sing, are all connected with the universal joy in God as Saviour and in His accomplishment of mighty saving acts for His people. Passages which speak of the establishment of the Kingdom of God and do not mention Messiah usually contain these references to the joy of the natural world at God's redeeming work. The Hebrew seems to have had little appreciation of the beauties of Nature, but a great appreciation of the Beauty of the LORD, and this latter is usually associated with His mighty saving acts. The abundant joy and fertility which will accompany the reconciliation of God and Israel is here (verses 22-3) connected with the name Jezreel. In 1⁴ Hosea made this name a threat of disaster and used its historical association. But now he uses its actual meaning, which is 'God sows'. 'The clouds ye so much dread are big with mercy' (*MHB* 503). The same God who is full of judgement for the unrepentant sinner is full of mercy for the repentant sinner. Man's repentance in response to God's call can turn the Jezreel of dread into the Jezreel of blessing. It is a mistake to say only that God is a God of love; He is both a God of judgement and a God of

love. Which men find Him to be depends upon the men.
Those who persist in evil ways find Him to be a God of
Judgement, stern and hard; those who turn to Him in repentance, earnestly desiring to be free from sin, find Him to be a
God of infinite love and compassion. We must not be senti-
mental about God's love. The condition of acceptance into
being right with God is Repentance and Faith, that is, full
sorrow for sin, a determination to follow in His way, and a
complete trust in Him which will enable us to do this; there
is no other way. The Cross makes this way open. It does not
open any other way; it makes this one way plain.

3^{1-5}: Israel's probation

The prophet is told to buy an adulteress to be his wife. He
does this, but isolates her for many days; no one, not even
Hosea himself, is to have relations with her. The prophetic
message which arises from this is given in 3^{4-5}. Israel will be
many days isolated from state and religion, but ultimately the
North will be reunited with the South in true worship of
Yahweh under a king of the line of David.

3^1. Hosea is to love the wayward woman just as God loves
wayward Israel. '*Cakes of raisins*' were apparently well-
pressed blocks of raisins (dried grapes). They were used in
religious feasts, apparently (as here) in Canaanite cults, and
also in the true Yahweh worship which the Chronicler knew
(1 Chr 16^3).

3^2. The dry measure '*homer*' is usually estimated as being
equivalent to eleven bushels, and was probably originally an
ass's load of barley. The term *lethek* is traditionally said to be
a half-homer.

3^4. The '*pillar*' was of stone, familiar in early times as a
dwelling-place for the deity. Stones seem to have been
regarded as legitimate in Yahweh worship until they were
prohibited in Deuteronomy (16^{22}), though in earlier times
the Canaanite pillars were to be destroyed (Ex 23^{24}, 34^{13}). The
'*ephod*' was an image (Judg 17^5) and was used in divination
(1 Sam 23^9). This ephod is distinct from the linen ephod
which the priests wore, and also distinct from the ephod of the

high priest of post-exilic times. The '*teraphim*' were images of
ancestors (Gen 31¹⁹, 1 Sam 19¹³) and these also were used in
divination (Ezek 21²¹, Zech 10²).

There is much dispute concerning this chapter, both as
regards the authorship, the date, and the meaning of the
details. The meaning of the whole is plain. It envisages a long
period of exile and isolation, but an ultimate return and a
restoration of the full Davidic kingdom embracing both
North and South. Some scholars think that the woman is
Gomer, whom they assume to have been divorced and to have
become a slave. In this case the whole chapter is from Hosea,
except the last half of verse 5 from '*and David their king*', the
assumption here being that no true Northerner would ever
look for a renewal of the former near-slavery of Solomon's
time. There is no reason to suppose that Hosea necessarily
regarded the king, the prince and the cult objects of verse 4
as being bad things. Our view, however, is that the whole
chapter is late, and that a late author is working out an
allegory based on the details of Hosea's life. Verse 4 contains
a list of bad things, comparable with the other gods and
heathen raisin-cakes of verse 2. Israel will be isolated from
all these bad things of Canaan, and ultimately will return to
be built up into the restored kingdom of David. Medieval
Jewish commentators say that '*in the latter days*' always
means 'in the days of the Messiah'.

4¹⁻³: Israel's moral corruption

God has a charge to make against the Israelites. There is no
true religion to be found in the land, but every kind of lawlessness and immorality. This is why they are having the long
drought, when every living thing, man, beast, bird and fish,
will suffer and pine away.

4². '*break out*' means either '*break all bounds*' (*RSV*) or 'break
in' as a burglar (cf. Job 24¹⁶). For '*blood toucheth blood*', the
Adult School translation has 'murder follows hard on murder',
which is an excellent rendering, because the Hebrew really
means 'bloodshed'.

4⁴⁻¹¹: The priests are responsible

In some of these verses the Hebrew is uncertain, though the

general sense is usually clear. It is no good, says Hosea, for one man to blame another. The priests are to blame. Priest and prophet alike will stumble, and the people with them because they have had no chance to know better. The priests have refused to know God; He will refuse to recognize them as priests. They have forgotten God; He will forget the whole priesthood. The greater they became (verse 7) in influence or numbers, the worse they became. They make money out of the false religion of the people and encourage them in it. People and priest alike will pay the penalty.

4⁴. The Hebrew of the last half of the verse is uncertain, and perhaps we should read '*for with you is my contention, O priest*' (*RSV*).

4⁵. Attached to the local shrines in pre-exilic times were prophets and priests, all of them cult officials, who cared for the shrine and gave oracles, each group after its own fashion. These professional, official prophets are to be distinguished from such men as Amos and Hosea, but Elijah and Elisha seem to be a link between the two types.

Hosea's tirade against the priest arises from the fact that the worship at the shrines was mixed worship of Baal and Yahweh. Perhaps they identified the two; more likely they thought they could worship both, just as the Canaanites could worship more than one god. In any case, the worship at the shrines involved sacred prostitution, and the conduct demanded was of a far lower level than that which such prophets as Amos and Hosea realized that Yahweh required. It was all due to lack of real knowledge of God. Yahweh of old laid down the laws which Israel was to obey. He may or may not have given instructions concerning ritual observances, but He certainly laid down rules of conduct, and these Canaanite habits flatly contradict them. What God requires is laid down by Hosea in 1¹⁹, and nothing less than this will suffice. The priest who does not both declare and himself fulfil this is no priest at all.

4¹²⁻¹⁴: Widespread apostasy

The people seek divine advice from wooden posts. The men are as bad as the women; there would not be any harlots if

there were no men who consorted with them. A people that
will not think and face the facts is doomed.

4¹². '*the spirit of whoredom hath caused them to err*'. The use
of the word '*spirit*' is important, for the Hebrew word (*ruach*)
usually denotes strength, power. It means the strong, rushing
wind as against the pleasant evening breeze. It stands for
power, and when used, as here, in a psychological sense, it
denotes some overpowering desire (see Num 5¹⁴ and the
phrase '*spirit of jealousy*'). Indeed, when any one is jealous,
it seems as if some power has seized hold of him and is driving
him headlong. He will not listen to reason. The power of sin
is like this. Men and women can be so much under the power
of sin that they find they are unable themselves to break its
bonds. The strength of desire can become so strong by repeated encouragement and indulgence that a man can be fast
bound in evil habits. Nothing except the saving power of God
in Christ can break these bonds. It is therefore proper to
talk of being saved from sin. The habit of inbred sin can be
so strong that a man cannot rescue himself from it; he must
be rescued by someone else. But Christ can break 'the power
of cancelled sin', and set 'the prisoner free' (*MHB* 1).

4¹⁵⁻¹⁹: A little miscellany

A warning to Judah (verse 15*a*): keep away from these idolatrous shrines (verse 15*b*); Israel is a mad heifer running wild;
how can God leave her to roam at large like a lamb in a wide
pasture? Israel is joined to her idols; leave her alone. The
wind will snatch her up and whirl her away; they will be sorry
they ever relied on their sacrifices. We have omitted verse 18; it
is untranslatable as it stands, and any restoration is conjectural.
The Adult School translation of verse 19 has 'will snatch her
up like a dust-devil', that is, like a column of dust driven along
in a whirling spiral.

5¹⁻⁷: Wholesale apostasy

The whole country, priests, rulers and people, has turned away
from Yahweh. These verses condemn them all. The following
is a translation, with occasional emendations where the
Hebrew is corrupt. 'Listen to this, you priests; pay attention,

you Israelites; hearken, you courtiers; for it is you that the verdict concerns. You have been a snare at Mizpah, a fowler's net spread out on Tabor. They have deepened the pit of Shittim (Num 25¹⁻⁹), and I will scourge all of them. I know Ephraim, and Israel cannot hide herself from me. You, Ephraim, have committed adultery; Israel has defiled himself. Their own habits will not let them turn back again to their God. A spirit of harlotry is in their midst, and they do not know Yahweh. The Pride of Israel (i.e. Yahweh) has testified plainly to Israel. Ephraim is brought down by her iniquity. (Judah also is brought down with them.) With their sheep and their oxen they come to seek Yahweh with their sacrifices, but they cannot find Him. He has withdrawn Himself from them. They have cheated Yahweh; they have borne half-caste children. A month will mean the end of them and their fields.'

5⁸⁻¹⁴: Disaster comes

The alarm is sounded; Gibeah, Ramah, Bethel (Bethaven) and Benjamin are called to arms. But disaster is certain. The princes of Judah are rogues and cheats. Ephraim is overthrown and crushed, because he preferred to follow vain idols. It is I, Yahweh, who am eating up Israel like a moth, and I am like dry-rot in Judah. When they saw how serious was their plight, they sent to the Great King of Assyria. He cannot heal or cure you, because I am your enemy. Like a strong lion I will maul you, carry you off, and no one will be able to rescue you.

5¹⁵-6⁶: Can Israel's repentance be genuine?

5¹⁵. Yahweh returns to His heavenly dwelling-place to wait for Israel's repentance under the stress of disaster. But when Israel turns to God in penitence (6¹⁻³), how can God be sure that it will last? Israel has always been fitful in her loyalty to Yahweh, unstable in her affections, and that is why, time and time again, His words have brought disaster, and His justice has been a thunder-bolt.

The first three verses of Chapter 6 are the words of repentant Israel. He has mauled us, but it was only to heal us; smitten us, but it was only to bind our wounds. In two or three days,

He will revive us and help us on to our feet, that we may live in His presence. Let us know Him, chase after Him to know Him. If we seek Him early enough and keenly enough, we shall find Him. He will come like the spring-rains which soak the soil (the March-April showers that ensure the new growth of the spring).

Repentance that rises out of trouble may or may not be true repentance. What is needed is not sorrow because of sin's results, but godly sorrow for sin. Israel's repentance, says Hosea, was never true repentance. Her loyalty ('*goodness*', 'kindness', *RV*m) lasted only for a little while, like morning clouds and morning dew which soon disappear as the sun regains his strength. Bringing sacrifices and whole-offerings is not enough. What is needed is steadfast loyalty, steadfast love ('*mercy*', *EVV*) and true knowledge of God (cf. Ps 51[10], Joel 2[13] ('*rend your heart, and not your garments*'), and Jer 4[4], where the circumcision which avails is not the outward circumcision of the flesh, but the inner circumcision of the heart). What is needed is 'true belief and true repentance' (*MHB* 324). It has been said that the prophets have no cure for sin, but can only exhort men to repent. This is far less than the truth. In passages like this, prophets and psalmists realize that the problem of sin is deep down in the heart of man. They realize (Jer 31[33]) that God's law must be written on man's heart, and that every man himself must know God and experience His indwelling. But we have to wait for the Redemption of the Cross before the solution of man's persistent waywardness is found. Man must be made anew; and '*if any man is in Christ, he is a new creation*' (2 Cor 5[17]).

Some scholars have seen in 6[6] evidence that the prophets were wholly against the sacrificial ritual. This is partly because they are predisposed to find such evidence, and partly because they are ignorant of Hebrew syntax. A literal English translation does indeed apparently deny that God desires sacrifices. Perhaps this is true, but it is not what Hosea says; the Hebrew means that God regards steadfast love and knowledge of Himself as being more important than sacrifice. When we consider the verse in the whole context of 5[15]–6[6], we can see that Hosea is speaking against the prevalent attitude that sacrifice and all the outward trappings of religion are sufficient. He is insisting that, if they do indeed come to God with their sacrifices and liturgical forms of penitence, they must come with truly penitent hearts. He is insisting that religion concerns the deepest depths of man's nature, and that outward forms by themselves are a deadly hindrance and no aid to getting right with God. Nobody can dispute this, whether he be ritualist or puritan. It is probable that both Jeremiah (7^{22}) and Amos (5^{25}) held that the sacrificial system of Solomon's temple had no place in the original Yahweh worship, but all the prophets agree that steadfast love and true knowledge of God are essential. The other may be a help, but it can be a hindrance.

6^{7-10}: Israel's repentance is mere feigning

Israel's sorrow for sin is not even skin-deep. The Hebrew in this section and the next is very difficult, and even the general sense of the passages is doubtful; the text here is the least well preserved of any part of the Old Testament. '*Like Adam*' (mortal man?) seems to be a corruption of some place-name.

6^8 may mean that Gilead is so full of evil-doers that you can track your way there by the blood of murdered men.

6^9 seems to mean that although Shechem was one of the cities of refuge where men who had accidentally killed someone could find safety, yet the gangs of priests there murdered such refugees wholesale.

6^{11a} is a threat against Judah, and is probably a later addition.

6^{11b} is to be taken with the next section.

$6^{11b}-7^7$: God knows Israel only too well

Every attempt of God's to bring Israel back to Him results in a further disclosure of her wickedness.

6^{11b}. Read 'when I (would) restore the fortunes of Israel'. There is complete confusion everywhere between the two phrases 'change the captivity' (*shub shebith*) and 'change the fortunes' (*shub shebuth*), partly because of their close similarity, and partly because during the Exile the one change of fortune which was desired above all others was the return from captivity (cf. especially Job 42^{10}, which must mean 'changed the fortunes of Job').

$7^{4, 6, 7}$. Here we find three metaphors drawn from the baker's oven, but each with a different significance.

7^4 says that the people are like a baker's oven with the fire damped down while the baker is waiting for the fermentation to take place. The implication is that as soon as the fermentation is complete the baker will stir up the fire and they will find themselves in the flames.

7^6 pictures a baker's oven with the fire damped down overnight, but blazing up as soon as the baker stirs it in the morning; that is, although there are times when their wickedness seems to abate, there is no real reformation, and soon they are worse than before.

7^7 says they are burning hot like a baker's oven, and will burn up anything and everything within their reach—look how they keep on murdering their kings, one after another. In 747 B.C., they had three kings, and two of them were murdered.

7^8: Ephraim is a cake not turned

The attempts to interpret this verse are almost as innumerable as the sand on the sea-shore. Here is another attempt. Perhaps it means that Ephraim is like 'marble-cake', not improperly baked because it is 'not-turned-over', but improperly mixed because the dough is not turned round enough, with the result that the cake is all streaky. Ephraim is all mixed up with foreign ideas and worship of foreign gods, and she is patchy, with here a little patch of Yahweh-worship, and there a whole wedge of false Baal-worship. Many of us are like that, good in patches and bad in patches, inconsistent, not always living up to the proper standard, having all sorts of curious lapses and blind patches. Other people see the bad patches more easily than we do ourselves, and thus through our blindness we can bring the Church of God into disrepute. The mire of the pit out of which we have been digged clings to us.

7^{9-16}: Beyond hope of redemption

Hosea continues with his catalogue of those developed

weaknesses which make Israel unable to turn back to God in true repentance.

7¹⁰. '*The pride of Israel*' is Yahweh Himself.

7¹¹. A silly fluttering dove, flying first one way and then another. The foreign policy of the two kingdoms was almost always like this, relying now on Assyria, now on Egypt, and now on the one against the other.

7¹²ᵇ is unintelligible; *RSV* emends to '*I will chastise them for their wicked deeds*'.

7¹⁴ probably means: 'they howl beside their altars, and cut themselves (*RV*m: cf. 1 Kings 18²⁸) in order to ensure my good will for good harvests.'

7¹⁶. The first phrase is unintelligible; perhaps *RSV* is right: '*they turn to Baal*'. They are like a treacherous bow, one that will not shoot straight.

For '*rage*', read '*insolence*' (*RSV*).

8¹⁻³: The invasion begins

The Assyrian is an eagle (griffon vulture), swooping down on the Holy Land (cf. 9¹⁵). The people cry out to God and claim that they know Him, but they have broken the covenant, rebelled against His law, and rejected that which is good.

8¹. The idea of the '*covenant*' is one of the main motifs of the Bible. The Bible indeed consists of what we call the Old Testament and the New Testament, and *testamentum* is the Latin (Vulgate) translation of the Hebrew *berith* (covenant), that which is binding. The idea of the covenant is found in the earliest records. It appears in the southern tradition (Gen 15¹⁸), where God makes a covenant with Abraham, and with Israel at Sinai (Ex 34¹⁰). It appears in the northern tradition (Ex 19⁵), where God makes a covenant with Israel at Sinai. In the Deuteronomic tradition and in the Priestly Tradition the idea of the Covenant between Yahweh and Israel is much more strongly emphasized. In the earlier traditions the covenant is not materially different from that between other peoples and their gods: the people performed the necessary sacrifices, observed the ritual, and generally fulfilled what was commanded, while the god, on his part, watched over his people and gave them prosperity. Neither could properly exist without the other. The idea of the Covenant-God and His 'peculiar' (the Hebrew word means special possession) people comes in with Deuteronomy in the seventh century. Indeed, it is in Deuteronomy 10[8] that the phrase '*the Ark of the Covenant*' is first found. Previously it has been '*the Ark of Yahweh (God)*'. With Deuteronomy comes the idea of Election, that Yahweh chose Israel. And again, it is emphatically stated that God did not choose them because of what they were, because they were righteous (Deut 9[5]) or because they were many (Deut 7[7]); He chose them because of their fathers and His promises to them (Deut 4[37]), because He loved them (Deut 7[8]). As Psalm 44[3] puts it, He saved them '*because* [he had] *a favour unto them*'. It was all of grace. Here is the beginning of the stream which becomes a mighty flood in the New Testament, that Grace of God in Christ which flows fully and freely to all. In the Priestly Code, we have another influence at work, and the covenant becomes closely allied with circumcision (Gen 17[10]) and with the Sabbath (Ex 31[16]), but this belongs to the days when Jewry was building '*the middle wall of partition*' around itself. Jesus seems to have had least interest in the Priestly traditions of the Pentateuch and most interest in Deuteronomy.

8[4-14]: Artificial kings and artificial gods[1]

The whole of this chapter is made up of short, violent sentences. It is disjointed, either because it is a collection of very short oracles, or because the prophet is so overwrought that he sweeps along like the whirlwind and the storm which he mentions in verse 7.

8[4]. Retain the text of *RV*. The last phrase probably refers to the idols being destroyed, though some take it to refer to the people either being destroyed or being cut off from Yahweh.

The commentators vary in their interpretation of this verse. Some think that the reference is to the break-away of the Northern Kingdom at the death of Solomon. Others think of

---

[1] George Adam Smith.

the many dynasties who ruled in the North—ten different dynasties in 253 years, and every one of them ended in murder and violence.

8⁵. Read 'I have cast off (spurned)'. It is best to take the first phrase of verse 6 with verse 5; but read 'in Israel' (so the Greek). The passage then runs: 'how long will they not be capable of innocency in Israel?'

Yahweh rejects the bull-cult of Samaria as being no worship of Him at all. The bull was connected in Israelite tradition with the golden calf of the Wilderness (Ex 32). The Rabbis said that in every sin there is something of the golden calf. The root of sin is the setting up by man of an image he has made himself. He thinks he can make god. He sets up other ideals; he seeks his happiness in other things; he trusts in other things. He makes God in his own image. Perhaps that is why he is so ready to worship the gods of his own creation. But there is something else in the bull-cult of Samaria. The high-god of Canaan (El) was worshipped in the image of a bull; he is often called 'the Bull-El'. So that there is also a reference here to a revival, or more likely a continuance, of the old Canaanite cults, a new apostasy which is a revival of the ancient waywardness.

8⁶. The first half of the rest of the verse reads: 'and it, a workman made it, and not a god is it' (cf. Isa 40¹⁹, 41⁷, 46⁶).

8⁷. The last two lines are terse and barely translatable. The standing corn has no growing point, it cannot produce flour; if it could, foreigners would gobble it up.

cf. Gal 6⁷, 2 Cor 9⁶, Rom 6²³. This world is dominated by justice, strict and hard, inexorable. Every deed inevitably brings its own harvest, and the harvest is gathered in full. But we are all bound together in one bundle of life, and we all share both for weal and for woe.

8⁸. Israel is gobbled up. The metaphor suddenly changes: other countries think no more of them than they do of cheap, coarse pottery.

8⁹ refers to Israel making advances to Assyria and bribing her for help. There is a pun in the Hebrew on '*Ephraim*' and '*wild* *ass'* (*pere*); the significance of this metaphor elsewhere is independence (Gen 16¹²).

8¹⁰ in the Hebrew is incomprehensible, but according to the ancient Greek Version, the latter half refers to the exile: 'they will cease for a little while from anointing kings and princes'. Perhaps the first half means 'when they give bribes to the foreigner, they will be gathered in with the bribes.'

8¹¹. The more altars Israel has built, the farther they have led him away into sin.

8¹². If I were to write down for him ten thousand things out of my Law, Israel would think it was all foreign; so little does he know of my true religion.

8¹³ is uncertain. Apparently it means: they love the sacrificial meals, when they can eat meat to their hearts' content. But such rites give Yahweh no pleasure; He does not accept such goings-on as true religion; there is no communion with God there. Punishment is coming: a return to the Egyptian captivity.

The sacrifices mentioned here are the sacrificial meals, of which almost the whole was eaten by the worshippers. All authorities are agreed that the rite was a communion meal. Some say the worshippers shared it with the god, and so strengthened the mutual bonds; others say the food was regarded as holy food, and the worshippers 'ate the god'. In either case, the communal meal was intended to be what has been called 'a means of grace' (see note on Amos 5²²). Hosea charges the people of his day with making it an occasion for gluttony and excess. They use the sacred meal for their own ends and enjoyment. Zechariah made a similar charge against the people of his day in the matter of fasting (Zech 7⁹). All worship can be misused in this way. If a church is built in ornate and luxurious fashion, for whose enjoyment is it so decorated? For God's, or for the worshippers? If a man says that he has a good time in a prayer-meeting, does he mean that he has enjoyed himself, or does he mean that the prayer has brought him nearer to God? If a hearer has enjoyed a sermon, does he mean that he has found personal satisfaction in listening, or does he mean that he has found new 'joy in the

Lord'? If a preacher has 'a good time', does he mean that he
has enjoyed preaching, or that he has reason to believe he has
brought men nearer to God? Even self-denial contains this
snare; the ascetic may enjoy the self-denial, and the martyr
can find a strange joy even in the pain of his martyrdom. This
form of masochism, delight in self-inflicted pain, is actually a
refined form of salvation by works, all the more dangerous
because it looks so much like absolute and complete self-
sacrifice. It is the devil's trap for those who at first resist
temptation—like the feigned retreat of William of Normandy
at Senlac (Hastings) when the Saxons had so far beaten back
his frontal attacks. The Saxons thought the Normans were
in full retreat and streamed out from their fortified position;
their initial success was thus the very means of their final dis-
comfiture. This self-denial, which is really a form of self-
gratification, is illustrated by the fasting mentioned in Isa
58$^{1-8}$, where real fasting is said to involve giving bread to the
hungry, bringing in the outcast, clothing the naked, and setting
the prisoners free.

8^{14}. The fact of the matter is that Israel has forgotten the God
that made him. The two kingdoms, Israel and Judah, have
built palaces and fortified cities and put their trust in them
instead of in God. He will destroy cities and palaces alike.

9$^{1-8}$: Harvest revels

Much of this section is difficult, and slight emendations have
to be made in the Hebrew. Much of the confusion in the text
is earlier than the old Greek translation. The harvest festivals
(barley at Easter, wheat at Whitsun, vintage at the Harvest
Full Moon) were celebrated with exuberant joy and (especially
the vintage) with abandoned revelry. Hosea describes them
all as the wages of harlotry, because Israel, the 'wife' of
Yahweh, has consistently misconducted herself with Baal.
The joy will be short-lived. Israel will get no good from them.
Either Egypt or Assyria will conquer the country and deport
the people. Then Israel will not be able to worship Him at all,
and all their religious feasts will have no purpose other than
the satisfaction of greedy, lustful appetites.

9^{4}. Israel will not pour out wine as a drink-offering to Yahweh, nor will they prepare their sacrificial feasts for Him. Their bread will be like mourners' bread (mourners were unclean and could not partake in worship; they were cut off from communion with Yahweh during the mourning period): all that eat it will be ritually unclean. Their food will be solely to gratify their appetites; it will not come to Yahweh's House.

9⁵. That will mean the end of the festivals and of the great autumn pilgrimage.

9⁶. For, behold, they will assuredly go to Assyria, and Egypt will gather them and Memphis bury them. Weeds will overgrow their precious silver idols, and thorns will grow in their sanctuaries (lit. 'tents').

9⁷ is difficult. Perhaps it should be understood thus: Hosea declares that the time of penalty and retribution has come, and Israel will know it. The people say: 'The prophet is a fool, the inspired man is mad'; to which Hosea replies: 'You are saying this because of your many iniquities and your great animosity against me.'

9⁸ could then continue: 'The prophet [i.e. Hosea himself] is Ephraim's watchman with his God: they lay traps for him on every road; there is animosity against him in the house of his god [i.e. among the official priests and prophets].'

All the three great feasts were harvest festivals, and harvest festivals are necessarily pilgrimages, when men bring the firstfruits to God at His shrine (see the comments on Amos 4⁴⁻⁵).

9⁹: The ancient crime

Ephraim-Israel's corruption is as deep as that of Benjamin and the atrocity of Judges 19. Retribution will follow now as surely as it did then.

9¹⁰⁻¹⁴: The fruitful becomes unfruitful

These verses depend for their meaning on the popular explanation of the name Ephraim, which was said to mean 'fruitful' (Gen 41⁵²).

9¹⁰. '*Like grapes in the wilderness*': unexpected, the last place in the world where we should expect to find them.

'*the firstripe*' fig is the best and sweetest of all (Isa 28⁴, Mic 7¹, Jer 24²).

'*Baal-peor*' is short for Beth-baal-peor, the house (temple) of the Baal of Peor; in Deuteronomy 3²⁹ the name is given as Beth-peor (see Num 25).

'*consecrated*'. This is the same root as the word Nazirite. The word has to do with the making of a vow, especially involving the hair. The Nazirite let his hair grow long, and his head of hair was sacred (tabu). In Israel all sacred persons never cut or shaved their hair. Kings wore a fillet (the same word is used for 'consecration', 'crown', 'Naziriteship') to keep their hair out of their eyes in battle, and this is probably the origin of the royal crown.

'*the shameful thing*'. The scribes who copied and preserved the Old Testament sometimes substituted the word *bosheth* (as here) for the heathen name 'baal': e.g. Ishbosheth for Ishbaal (see note on Amos 5²⁵). All this was to show their hatred of idolatrous names, and perhaps also to prevent the reader pronouncing the wicked word. There is something to be said for avoiding even the appearance of evil. The wise man is he who keeps farthest away from temptation.

9¹³. The reference to '*Tyre*' and '*planted in a pleasant place*' is incomprehensible. It is best to follow the Greek Version and to read 'Ephraim, as I have seen, is destined for game (i.e. animals or birds shot by the hunter or caught in snares), bereft of her sons', continuing with the idea that all the sons Ephraim produces are doomed to slaughter.

9¹⁵⁻¹⁷: Miscellaneous couplets

9¹⁵. Yahweh declares that the root of the trouble is to be found in the Gilgal sanctuary.

9¹⁶. Hosea returns to the theme of Ephraim meaning 'fruitful'.

9¹⁷. A renewed threat of exile.

10¹⁻²: The religion of the prosperous

The first line of verse 1 is difficult, though the general meaning is clear. Israel is a luxuriant vine, steadily and rapidly growing more and more luxuriant and producing abundant fruit. The policy is: more fruit, more altars, better land, better pillars. But (verse 2) Israel is divided in purpose and loyalty (cf. 1 Kings 18[21]), trying to worship both Yahweh and Baal—the Yahweh who brought them through the desert into Palestine, and the Baal whom the Canaanites worshipped as the Rider of the Clouds.

10[2]. '*found guilty*'. This translation is not adequate. The word means 'pay up', 'pay the equivalent of'. The noun is usually translated 'guilt-offering'. Actually this was never an offering in the sense of something given to God, but only in the sense of something brought into the Temple and used in the ritual; it was a compensation payment in cases where the damage done could be assessed (cf. Isa 53[10], where '*when thou shalt make his soul an offering for sin*' actually means 'when you recognize that his life was given instead of yours'). Here in Hosea the meaning is: Israel must pay the price for her double-mindedness, and Yahweh will tear down and destroy altars and pillars.

The metaphor of the vine as descriptive of Israel is well-established and widespread. This is one of the earliest uses of it, possibly it is the earliest, but the popularity of the figure of speech may be due rather to Isaiah's use of it in his elaborate allegory in Isa 5[1-7], with the particular statement in verse 7. See also Psalm 80[8-19] and Jer 2[21] (originally a true strain, but turned into the suckers of a foreign vine—i.e. the graft has died and the old heathen stock has made vigorous growth). Another important passage is Deuteronomy 32[32], because this Deuteronomic Song of Moses is an ancient pre-Christian Sabbath Canticle, and (like its parallel Song of Moses in Ex 15) is still so used. The '*shoot out of the stock of Jesse*' (Isa 11[1]) and '*the Branch*' (Jer 23[5], Zech 3[8]) are both figures from the culture of the vine. Nothing looks so dead as last year's vine-stock; but as soon as the new growth begins, nothing is more eloquent of vigour and life. Thus the Shoot, the Branch, is a name for Messiah. Jesus is the true vine, the true stock of Israel, the true shoot out of the stock of Jesse. In the Temple of Jesus' time, there was a gigantic golden vine over the porch which was in front of the Holy of Holies; it had clusters of grapes hanging down as large as a man. This golden vine was so placed that the worshippers would be able to peer through the Gate of Nicanor and see it beyond the rising smoke of the sacrifices. This reference in the Fourth Gospel (Jn 15[1]) is one of several which apparently are based on knowledge of the Temple and its services, especially at Feast-times.

10[3-4]: No king, but kings were never any good

These two verses are difficult. The Hebrew makes little sense, and whilst the Greek makes better sense, it is difficult to be sure of the precise meaning. If the two couplets belong to Hosea, he means 'we have no real king, because we have not revered Yahweh. What does the king do for us? Nothing but talk, make false oaths, make and break treaties as he pleases, and his justice is just about as useful as poisonous weeds in the furrows of the farmland.' The couplets may, however, be later than Hosea, and mean 'we have no king now, and if we had he would be no good. . . .'

10[5-8]: The end of idol and idolators

These verses are badly preserved. Probably the meaning is: the inhabitants of Samaria will mourn for the calf of Beth-aven (i.e. Bethel); its people will mourn for it, and its priests be in agony for its splendour which will have been taken away to exile. For it will be taken to Assyria, as tribute to the Great King. Ephraim will be shamed, Israel will be ashamed of its diplomacy (so Adult School Translation). Samaria will be destroyed; her king will be swept away like a twig on a stream. Verse 8 as *RV*, *AV*.

10[9-10]: Retribution

Again, these verses are most uncertain. Perhaps they should read: 'Ever since the days of Gibeah you have sinned, O Israel. Shall not war overtake them in Gibeah? I will come against the lawless ones and punish them. Peoples will be gathered against them when they are punished for their two wicked deeds.'

It is uncertain what is meant by Israel's two wicked deeds. One of them is apparently the ancient horror of Gibeah, to which Hosea has already referred (9[9]); the other is probably the bull worship of Bethel, which the prophet regards as a modern version of the old wickedness. Some scholars think the reference is to the bull-worship and to the monarchy, but all is uncertain.

10^{11-12}: Hard work is the cure

'Ephraim is a domesticated heifer, she loves threshing (easy work), and I have spared her lovely neck (not yoked her to hard work). Now I will make Ephraim do heavy draught work. Judah must plough; Jacob must harrow. Sow righteousness for yourselves; reap the harvest of steadfast loyalty (Hebrew: *chesed*, see 2^7). Break up your fallow land; it is time to seek Yahweh that He may come and rain salvation upon you (? teach you honesty).'

Israel's easy prosperity has led her into easy ways. If she is going to avoid the imminent disaster which easy-going optimism brings, then there is need for stern moral discipline. What men sow, that they also reap. General laxity when all is going well gives an appearance of freedom to all, but no nation can survive without the basic virtues of right action and steadfast loyalty. It is necessary that men shall be able to trust each other, that there shall be give-and-take and mutual consideration. No society of men can survive without these. Hosea and the prophets base these social virtues, not on any barely humanitarian principles, but on the Nature of God Himself. The 'righteousness' which Israel must sow and cultivate is not the 'good for man', nor is it 'man's highest good'; it involves conforming to those more-than-ethical demands which form the distinctive element in the teaching of the prophets.

10^{13-15}: Bad seed, worse harvest

Israel has done the precise opposite of what is said in 10^{12}. Disaster will assuredly come. It is best to follow the ancient Greek Version in verse 15: 'so shall I do to you, O Israel . . .'. If 'in the daybreak' is correct, the meaning is that the king of Israel will be destroyed and will vanish like a dream on waking.

11^{1-9}: God's dilemma

God loved Israel as a child, and called him out of Egypt to adopt him as His son. But the more He called them, the farther the people went away from Him. But He taught them to walk, and when they fell, He picked them up in His arms, He kissed them better, and they never realized that they had been hurt. The figure now changes, and we have the picture of the owner leading a draught animal by a rope. It was a rope of love and . . . (the rest of the verse makes no sense, and the text was already corrupt in the time of the Greek translators; the sense appears to be that God was a humane master who lifted the yoke off from the animal's jaws (?) at feeding time).

11⁵. The negative is not in the Greek and should be omitted. The prophet is once more speaking of the coming exile, either in Egypt or in Assyria.

11⁶ tells of the coming devastation.

11⁷ is uncertain, and any attempted translation is largely guesswork.

11⁸ portrays God's dilemma: He must allow the seed of wickedness to ripen into a harvest of woe. His love for Israel is still as strong and steadfast as ever. What can He do?

11⁹ may mean 'I will not execute the full fierceness of my anger, and completely destroy Ephraim'; or it may be a question: 'Am I to destroy Ephraim in spite of my continued steadfast love?' The last phrase of the verse is unintelligible. The middle portion is a declaration of God's transcendence: He is God and not man; He is the Holy One in Israel's midst.

These verses bring into the forefront God's great problem in dealing with man's sin. The whole history of Israel has been the story of continued love and care on God's part, and persistent waywardness on Israel's part. He taught the tiny child to walk and healed all childhood's cuts and bruises; but the more He did for Israel, the more wayward Israel became. Admah and Zeboim are two of the cities of the plain, which were destroyed with Sodom and Gomorrah (Deuteronomy 29²³). What is God to do in the last resort? The problem is still with us. God demands godly-living, right action, truth and loyalty, and nothing that is alien to Him can have any place in His kingdom. There must therefore be judgement and condemnation. There is the 'outer darkness' (Mt 22¹³, 25³⁰), and there comes a time when the door is shut (Mt 25¹⁰) and 'I know you not' (Mt 25¹²). On the other hand, God is a God of love and He saves to the very uttermost (Jn 3¹⁶, etc.). Are some eternally lost? Or are all saved at last? If Hosea 11⁹ is a question, then Hosea is as uncertain as many modern people. In any case, the practical issue for men and women is to be found in the teaching of Matthew 25 and in 2 Corinthians 6².

11¹⁰⁻¹¹: Later—the exiles return

These two verses seem to be a later addition by a writer who could not bring himself to believe that God would cast Israel off at last. The metaphors are considerably confused. Yahweh will roar like a lion, and the people will follow after Him; children will come trembling from the west, like sparrows from Egypt and doves from Assyria, and He will bring them back home (Hebrew has 'enable them to dwell').

11¹²⁻12¹⁴: Many voices

This, which comprises Chapter 12 in the Hebrew, is a confused chapter. It is best to think of 11¹², 12¹⁻³ᵃ, 12⁷⁻¹¹, 12¹⁴ as the original, and the rest (12³ᵇ⁻⁶, 12¹²⁻¹³) as two insertions which deal with Jacob-Israel in a favourable light, in contrast with the devastating criticism of the original verses.

Jacob always was a 'heel'. The slang word gives the precise meaning of the Hebrew: in Genesis 25²⁶ the name 'Jacob' is connected with the Hebrew word 'heel', and means 'one who takes by the heel, attacks from behind', and so 'deceiver'. Jacob is his name, and Jacob is his nature. He is a true Canaanite (this word can mean 'trader' as well as inhabitant of Canaan) with loaded scales; there is nothing he likes better than to cheat at business. The first section of the insertion (verses 6*b*-3) is a similar treatment of Jacob's other name— Israel, 'the one who persevered with God', who 'prevailed with God' (Gen 32²⁸). It was at Bethel, says the writer, that Jacob found God, and there too God spoke with us. And you must turn back by God's help; keep faith with God and do His will, and wait on Him continually. The second section of the insertion (12¹²⁻¹³) is a rough analogy between Jacob keeping sheep in the Aramæan country, and God keeping Israel by a prophet.

13¹⁻¹⁵: The doom of Israel

Ephraim once was a prince in Israel, and men trembled when he spoke. But he became guilty through Baal and he is doomed. 'They say (verse 2, following the Greek): "Sacrifice to these"; and men kiss the calves.' The punishment will be swift, and sinners will be quickly swept away like morning mist and dew rapidly disappearing as 'the sun grows hot', like smoke drifting through the window and then suddenly whisked away as the wind catches it. God is One and all Alone: there is no idol (no other loyalty) for Israel, and no other Saviour, either in the desert or in Canaan. But they have turned away from Him, and He perforce has 'turned to be their enemy' (Isa 63¹⁰). Their kings and princes were a snare from first to last. Verses 12 and 13 are difficult; they possibly mean: Ephraim has been heaping up retribution all through the years, hidden and unrealized; the punishment will come with pain and suddenly; and when the time comes, he will not be able to stand when the hidden troubles come to birth. It is best to make verse 14 a series of questions, meaning 'shall I ransom them? No! . . . Come, death with your terrors and plagues.'

13⁴. *'no god but me'*; that is, if the above exegesis is right, no idol (no substitute of any kind), no other Saviour. There is no thing, no person, no institution, no book, no anything at all, except only God, whom we can trust. There is nothing at all which can be to any degree a substitute for the living God, who is to be known in the experience of trusting Him day by day and relying upon Him continually.

14¹⁻⁸: One last appeal

Some scholars think that this chapter is a later addition by a writer who could not bear to think that destruction and death were God's last word for Israel. But there is no necessity to deny these verses to Hosea, because the swift alternation between condemnation and exhortation to repentance is found everywhere in the book, reaching its peak in the dilemma of 11⁸.

14¹. For '*return*', read 'repent'; the name Shear-jashub (Isa 7³) does not mean 'a remnant shall return' in the sense of 'return from exile', but in the sense of 'return to God' (i.e. 'repent', as in *RV*m).

14². The '*words*' are to be words of confession. For '*so will we render . . .*' read 'so will we render as a thank-offering the fruit of our lips' (so the Greek).

14⁴. We will not look for help from Assyria, from Egypt, or from our idols.

Where there is true repentance, the iniquity is removed and God 'receives us graciously' (*RV*m). This was the symbolism of the sin-offering. The animal became the 'sin' and was taken away, disposed of, so that the sin no longer remained between man and God. For the animal which was the sin-offering did not go to the altar and was in no sense a gift to God; it was taken away, disposed of, either eaten by the priests and levites, or burned 'outside the camp'. If we realize how great and unswerving is God's love to us, then we know that if we are truly repentant the guilt is no longer lying between us and Him as a barrier against communion. The Cross is a demonstration of God's unfailing love, and part of its message and effectiveness is expressed by the idea that Christ became a sin-offering on our behalf to remove our sins and bring us close again to God.

14⁹: Conclusion

This final verse is an addition in the phraseology of the wise men of Israel. It expresses the double aspect of God's ways with men: strength and guidance for the loyal; trouble and disaster for the rebellious. Compare Luke 2³⁴, and also Luke 20¹⁸, which is based on Isaiah 8¹⁴: God is a sanctuary and also a stone of stumbling. There is always this double aspect in God's dealings with men: strict and stern justice, and everlasting love and mercy. To say that God is a God of righteousness and justice and to say no more than this is wrong. To say that God is a God of love who saves to the very uttermost and to say no more than this is equally wrong. Both statements together are right. The decisive point is man's repentance and faith. But is the final result in man's hands or in God's?

Micah

MICAH was a peasant from Moresheth of Gath. He is the William Langland of the Old Testament, and has grown impatient beyond all bearing against the wealthy excesses of the rich contrasted with the poverty of the peasant. He has no hope for the rich, and no hope for the city. The first three chapters are unanimously ascribed to him; but there is no unanimity concerning the rest of the book, though most of it seems to belong to roughly the same period. The prophet was a late contemporary of Isaiah of Jerusalem, and the period of his activity is usually given as from about 715 to 701 B.C. This would include Sennacherib's attack on Jerusalem in the reign of king Hezekiah, the occasion when the siege was mysteriously raised during the night, and Jerusalem was saved when everything seemed lost.

1¹: Introduction

Once more, as in Amos and Hosea, there is an editorial introduction, fixing the date of the prophet. Micah was active as a prophet in the time of Hezekiah (Jer 26¹⁸), but there is no evidence that he was busy as early as the time of Jotham, who was dead before 740 B.C. It is unlikely that Micah was active till at least the end of Ahaz's reign (about 725 B.C.).

1²⁻⁹: Down with the cities

Micah the countryman denounces the two capitals, Samaria and Jerusalem. Yahweh descends and declares that he will destroy Samaria. The prophet laments. The wave of the Assyrian invasion will reach the gates of Jerusalem.

The oracle is composed of six double-couplet strophes. Omit verse 7 as a later insertion; it is the only place where the idolatrous worship is condemned, and moreover, verse 8 can scarcely follow it, whereas verse 8 makes a perfect sequence to verse 6.

1². '*his holy temple*'. There is some evidence that this holy temple is in the heavens (Isa 63¹⁵, Ps 11⁴, and especially Amos 9⁶ with its picture of a great palace based on a mighty arch over the earth and towering up terrace after terrace above the clouds). But there is a strong popular tradition of a sacred mountain away in the far north (Zaphon). The road there is flanked by two great mountains ('*the sides of the north*'), and in Psalm 48¹ᶠ this imagery is used of Yahweh's earthly temple on Mount Zion. It is probable that the heavenly temple is that fabled to exist on Mount Zaphon, inaccessibly high above the clouds.

1³. The idea of God coming down and stamping down the mountains, melting them in the fiery heat of His presence and His anger against sin, is found more than once elsewhere (cf. Ps 18⁶⁻¹⁵ and margin refs). Micah gives the old phrases a new turn: '*the high-places of Judah*' means Jerusalem, the southern capital, just as the '*transgression*' (read 'rebellion') of Jacob is Samaria, the northern capital. Amos had a concern for the poor, and had much to say against the rich for their exploitation of the common man. In Micah there is the bitterness of generations of maltreatment. Much of what he says can be paralleled in the revolt of the common man all the world over which is a feature of this present post-war period. The sorrows of Micah and his peasant friends are the stuff out of which communism is made.

1⁵. For '*Israel*' read 'Judah', in view of the rest of the verse and its parallels.

1⁶. The occasion is probably the capture of Samaria in 722 B.C., and Sargon's march down the coast against Egypt. Micah thinks of the Assyrian king, after his defeat of Egypt, as turning east against Jerusalem, the usual avenue of attack (see verses 10-15), and the course of almost every assault in history against the city.

All the earth is called to listen and watch for God's testimony against Israel-Judah. This is the verdict of history, and all history is God's verdict on mankind. Some men see no pattern at all, some see the play of economic forces, some see the outworking of justice; others see the hand of the living God, alike in judgement and in salvation, condemning all sin of man and overthrowing pride, but showing mercy to the humble and giving strength to those who seek in Him their inspiration and power.

1¹⁰⁻¹⁶: Micah's lament

All these verses, except the last, describe the route of an army advancing from the Philistine country against Jerusalem. Most of them consist of plays on the sound of the place names: e.g. the word for '*dust*' (*'aphar*: **1¹⁰**) sounds very like the place name '*Beth-'aphrah*'. Gath had already been destroyed, and never recovered. '*Tell it not in Gath*' had already become proverbial as the opening of an elegy, because of 2 Samuel 1²⁰. All these places which can be identified are between the main road down to Egypt ('*the way of the land of the Philistines*', Ex 13¹⁷) and Jerusalem.

1¹⁵. If the reference to the cave of Adullam is correct, then we have an allusion to David's flight from Saul. The nobility of Israel will have to flee and hide away in the rough country of the far south.

1¹⁶. The shaving of the head was an ancient mourning custom, common in Old Israel. It was prohibited in the Deuteronomic legislation toward the end of the seventh century (Deut 14¹), but there is plenty of evidence that it was common in earlier days, and prophets like Amos (8¹⁰), Isaiah (3²⁴) and Micah (here) regard it as the perfectly normal and proper sign of mourning for the dead. The original idea behind it was to give what was living to the dead, because the hair was supposed to contain life to a special degree. The custom of giving hair to the dead is common throughout the world of primitive man. It was abolished in the attempt of Josiah and his supporters to do away with every vestige of Canaanite custom and religion in order to keep the religion and worship of Yahweh pure and uncontaminated. For '*eagle*' read 'vulture', because of its baldness. It is probable that the word here used (*nesher*) normally includes both eagle and vulture, but here it certainly means 'vulture' and not 'eagle'. See note on Amos 8¹⁰.

Almost all the ceremonies in one religion can be paralleled by similar ceremonies in others. These customs belong to 'natural religion', and apparently man's reaction to the spiritual world is much the same all the world over. The custom of turning to the east was originally a turning towards the rising sun, and it has been adopted by more than one religion in the form of turning to the sacred place of that religion; similarly, the custom of eating sacred meals can be found everywhere and goes back into the mists of antiquity; and so with all religious forms and ceremonies. There are two possible attitudes: either, use every means of expressing our devotion to God and of seeking to establish and maintain communion with Him (in which case, we must be most careful to know exactly what we are doing and why we are doing it, and our explanation must be definitely a Christian one); or, avoid all these customs as much as possible, because of the danger of debasing Christianity with non-Christian ideas and especially with those notions of magic (using God and compelling God) which are a feature of many religious cults. Josiah (621 B.C.) came to the conclusion that much of the ritual of his day was a snare, and he sought to abolish at least some of it. This is the attitude in Deuteronomy, which sought to cut out of Israelite life and religion all that it could of the old Canaanite traditions.

2^{1-11}: Oppression of the poor

It is here that Micah shows himself as the William Langland of the Old Testament. This is the *cri de coeur* of the peasant who has suffered from the rapacity of the rich. The big land-owners are crowding out the smallholder, driving him off his ancestral plot of land, reducing him to poverty, till he must work for the land-owner at whatever rates the land-owner fixes. The situation has its parallels in most countries: the enclosure of the common-lands in England, and the driving out of Scotland of the clansmen. The wealthy people (2^6) try to influence the prophet not to speak of such things ('Keep politics out of the pulpit'), but the prophet insists. He threatens them with exile (verse 10), and says that if the prophet preached about the excellencies of wines and beers, then doubtless they would be fully satisfied.

Notice the contrast between verse 1 and verse 3: the rich spend half the night in devising new schemes for robbing the poor; let them not forget that God is devising schemes also and they are the ones that are going to suffer. Presumably the yoke of verse 3 is exile and captivity, since deportation was the regular policy of both Assyria and Babylon when the first policy of ruling through a native puppet-king failed.

2⁴. The Hebrew is difficult, and the ancient Greek Version varies considerably from it, but it is just translatable. The rich now lament that they are completely robbed. The '*portion*' (the strip of land which belonged to one family and was part of the cultivated land round the village) will be taken away from them also, and the field (the cultivated land round the village) will be 'portioned off' among the captors (read this instead of '*rebellious*': see *RSV*).

2⁵. There will be no means by which the Judæans themselves will be able to portion out the 'field'.

2⁶. This verse is confused—the probable meaning is: Do not preach at all; nobody should preach about such things; disgrace will not reach us.

2⁷. Is the Spirit of God so short in its reach that it does not extend to conduct like this? God's active word benefits the upright, and actions of this type are not countenanced by Him.

2⁸. The difficulty of the Hebrew continues. Probably we should read (cf. *RSV*): 'but you (i.e. the land-grabbers) are rising up against my people as an enemy; you strip off the mantle from the peaceful passer by'. (The last two words are unintelligible, but may mean 'war-captive'.)

This oracle is directed against the land-grabbers on two counts: one, that they oppress the poor and seize his property; two, that they seek to stop the prophet saying anything about such conduct. Such conduct did not die with the death of Micah's opponents. Five of the six Tolpuddle martyrs who were sentenced at Dorchester in March 1838 were Methodists. The Wesleyan Church took no official part in the agitation which led to the release of the men after they had served half their seven years sentence in the chain gang in Tasmania or on the farms on the mainland. When they came home, official Wesleyan Methodism did nothing to help them, and it was left to a committee of the general public to find farms for the men. The story of the Tolpuddle martyrs is typical of the general official attitude of the Churches to these problems in time past. It is true that practically every social reform in this country has originated in the activity of Christian men and women who have done what they have done because they were Christians. It is also true that the Churches officially have been slow in matters of social reform. This is mainly the weakness of organizations; the advance is determined by the speed of the slowest member, that is, if the group is to hold together. The difference between a hundred-odd years ago and today is to be judged by the existence and the activities of the Methodist Christian Citizenship Department and the substance of the Conference Declarations. Christianity has a very great deal to do with social problems. The religion that is true and deals with the whole man must necessarily have something to say about all the affairs of men at all levels. Micah was right; the man who tries to keep his religion separate from his daily life ends up with a religion and a daily life that are concerned with nothing but himself. Such a man has no place in the world to come, however big and prominent a place he may occupy in this world. If such a man is a pillar of his Church, he must not be surprised if ordinary folk leave him to do all the supporting and keep clear altogether. Micah could see that such conduct would end in Zion being a ploughed field, that is, the Temple being entirely destroyed. That will be the end of any Church which seeks to avoid its Christian social responsibility.

2¹²⁻¹³: The return of the exiles

These two verses do not seem to belong to their context, and most scholars think of them as belonging to the period of the Exile, looking forward to a return to Jerusalem of the survivors. 'The breaker' is the leading ram of the flock, unless perchance the shepherd himself is meant. 'Their king' (verse 13) is either the Messianic king, the descendant of David in whom the kingdom will be restored, or (if we are to follow the usual parallel pattern of Hebrew poetry) God Himself (see the last line of verse 13).

2¹². The reference to Bozrah is difficult, since Bozrah was the later capital of Edom. A change in the vowels of the Hebrew word give the meaning 'in a sheep-fold', which makes much better sense and is probably right.

If the reference to 'men' at the end of the verse is to be

retained, we should read 'they shall hum with men' (George Adam Smith).

The Hebrew word for '*flock*' comes from a root which means 'lag behind'. We think of a flock as a crowded mass of sheep with the shepherd behind driving them on; the Bible picture is of the shepherd leading the way and the flock streaming on behind him (cf. Song 4¹, 6⁵, where the long streaming black hair of the maiden is compared to a flock of black-haired goats passing across the distant hill-side, and tailing out as the slower sheep lag behind). The reference to '*the remnant*' is one of the earliest uses of the twin words *she'ar* and *she'erith* as technical terms for the faithful nucleus of Israel. It is in the faithful remnant that again and again Yahweh has to fix His hopes for the future, and again and again it is through them that He carries on His saving work. The remnant is the '*salt of the earth*' (Mt 5¹³) which can preserve the whole. The remnant not only secures the maintenance of God's work and witness in the world, but can itself be the means of salvation. If there are only ten righteous men in Sodom, then Sodom will be saved (Gen 18³²). The idea of a small remnant which by its faithfulness can save the rest is thus declared very early in the Old Testament. The remnant is the means of God's work of salvation, regrettable in that it is only a small part of the whole, but a matter of joy in that however wayward the people may be, there will still be '*seven thousand in Israel*' that '*have not bowed unto Baal*' (1 Kings 19¹⁸). God, so to speak, is always having to start again—after the flood with Noah and his family, with Abraham, with Jacob, with Joseph-Ephraim-Israel, with Judah (Ps 78, especially verses 67f), with *the children of the captivity*' (Ezra 4¹⁻³, 8, etc.), then with the '*son of man*' (Dan 7¹³) who represents '*the saints of the Most High*' (Dan 7¹⁸, ²⁷). According to Dr T. W. Manson, this Remnant, the Son of Man, gets narrowed down at last to the Lord Jesus Himself alone, and then as from Pentecost begins to grow like the grain of mustard seed. When the vessel '*was marred in the hand of the potter, he made it again another vessel, as seemed good to the potter to make it* (Jer 18⁴). The danger of the Remnant-idea is that the nucleus should build walls round itself and be satisfied. The Remnant is not a safe enclave, but a cell in the modern propaganda sense, the seed of future growth, the restless shoot that must blossom and produce fruit. The Church is not an end in itself, but a means to an end. It must always be pushing down its walls and reaching out; its purpose is to bring '*a light to the Gentiles*' and God's '*salvation to the end of the earth*'. When the people of God ceases in any age to do this, God starts again with another remnant.

3^{1-8}: Down with princes and prophets

The leaders of the people are condemned because they 'skin' the poor. The prophets are condemned because they promise good fortune when they are feed and fed, and are altogether antagonistic to the man who does not fee and feed them. Their doom is that they will see no vision, nothing but darkness. But Micah declares that he himself is inspired of God with power to proclaim the rebellious sin of Israel and Judah.

3^8. It is practically certain that the phrase '*by the spirit of the LORD*' is an explanatory note inserted to explain the source of the prophet's power. The prophet is filled with power and judgement and might, and the note is perfectly sound, for the prophet is a prophet because he is possessed and controlled by the Spirit of God. This word *ruach* is variously translated by 'wind, breath, spirit'. When it is used of the wind, it indicates strong, powerful wind rather than a soft breeze; when it is used of breath, it means noisy breathing, as though 'out of breath' or under the stress of overpowering emotion (see the note on Hos 4^{12}). The New Testament development is that at Pentecost the dominant note in the descent of the Holy Spirit is one of power; it was like a mighty rushing wind. The disciples found themselves possessed by a power that was not their own. The Jewish Feast of Pentecost was thought of as the Day of Power, and had been recognized as the Day of Yahweh's coming in power for some generations before the time of our Lord. This is shown by the proper psalms and lessons for the day in the synagogues; they were Exodus 19, Habakkuk 3, Ezekiel 1, Psalm 29, in all of which there is mention of earthquake, great voices (thunders), and mighty power. There is also an ancient tradition of the Rabbis that the great voices heard on Sinai were seventy in number, according to the total number of nations believed to inhabit the earth. It will be seen that all these details are to be found in the description of the Descent of the Holy Spirit in Acts 2^{1-13}, except the earthquake; but for the earthquake, see the description of the gift of the Holy Spirit in Acts 4³¹. An examination of the hymns in *MHB* in the section 'The Holy Spirit: His person, mission and work' shows that this emphasis on power is clearer in some hymns than in others. The reference to the dove in *MHB* 276², is out of place in a Pentecost hymn, and the same applies to the second verse of *MHB* 283. One of the Pentecost hymns truest to the early tradition is *MHB* 284.

3⁹⁻¹²: The doom of Judah

Because of the iniquity and perversions of rulers, priests and prophets, Zion will be ploughed up, Jerusalem will become rubbish heaps, and the temple mount like a hill in the badlands.

3¹². '*forest*'. The Hebrew word does not refer to a forest, but to the 'bad-lands', rough country, sometimes wooded, but full of sudden chasms, and every kind of danger (see 2 Sam 18⁸: '*the forest*', i.e. the rough country—this is the old English meaning of the word. The New Forest was never all wooded, but rather 'rough country'—'*devoured more people that day than the sword devoured*'). These four verses saved Jeremiah's life (Jer 26¹⁸).

4¹⁻⁵: Yahweh, God of all the world

The first three verses are found, almost without variation, in Isaiah 2¹⁻⁴. All nations will stream to Zion to worship Yahweh in His Holy Temple. They will be eager to learn His ways and walk in the paths He directs. He will be the judge of all peoples, and the era of universal peace will begin. The conclusion varies. In Isaiah 2⁵ the house of Jacob is bidden to walk in the light of Yahweh. Here in Micah, the picture is that of the Syrian peasant's dream of ease and comfort, with the traditional phrases '*sit every man under his vine and under his fig tree*'. Compare the opening chapter in Marmaduke Pickthall's *Said the Fisherman*. Verse 5 is partly similar to Isaiah 2⁵, but it is also markedly different from it and from the oracle itself. It expects all the nations to walk each one in the way of its own god. Since this prophecy is found in two places, there has been much discussion as to its origin and date. The most likely solution is that it belongs originally neither to Micah nor to Isaiah, but is an anonymous contemporary oracle which both of them used, each adding his own conclusion. It is probable that the work of Micah of Moresheth-gath ends with 4^5, unless, as most suggest, it ends with Chapter 3.

Jerusalem and its Temple are envisaged as the rallying point of all nations. It will be the religious centre of the whole world. Men will bring all their disputes and differences of opinion to Jerusalem (verse 3) in order that an amicable settlement may be found. The Hague International Court, the League of Nations and the United Nations Organization have been established during this present century. Here is a prophet looking forward to such a means of world unity and peace, more than two thousand six hundred years ago. Some scholars have thought that the ideal protrayed in these verses must be too early for the eighth century B.C., but the objection is based on a false theory of evolutionary development. It is true that intellectual thought and scientific knowledge are in general matters of development, one idea growing out of another; though even in these realms there are flashes of inspiration which seem to come from somewhere outside any normal smooth development, 'emergents' of the Lloyd Morgan type in the world of thought. But in religious matters we believe there is such a thing as revelation from God of a type all its own. This means that there may come at any time in the history of man a thought, an idea, a new vision, which humanly speaking is thousands of years before its time. As Professor G. Ernest Wright says, speaking of the theories of monotheism as arising from animistic ideas and so forth: monotheism never came out of that sort of thing, it was a straight revelation from God. And so with ideas and visions such as this in Isaiah 2 and Micah 4; they are visions of God. But why is world unity so long delayed? The answer is that the Hague, Geneva, New York are not enough; the earnest hopes of man are not enough; human thoughts and aspirations are not enough—even the best and highest of them. The mountain to which the nations must come is the Mount of God. The way to universal brotherhood and peace is the path of God, and there is no other way. Leaders of the nations are fond of quoting the phrase 'men of goodwill'. That is the reading of the first great New Testament (uncial) manuscripts: 'peace on earth to men of goodwill' (Lk 2^{14}). But the word '*goodwill*' (margin 'good pleasure') does not mean man's goodwill. The Greek word stands for the old Hebrew word which is used predominantly for God's goodwill, getting right with God. The corresponding verb is used in Hebrew for getting right with God after paying the price of sin in suffering, or showing true repentance both by an inner change of heart and by outward signs and observances. The angels' song therefore says that peace comes on earth to men who first of all have got right with God. We must get right with God first, and then we can get right with man.

4⁴. The translators have added '*it*' at the end of the verse. There is no need for this, and indeed the verse is better without the addition (cf. *RSV*). A similar needless, and indeed erroneous addition has been made in Isaiah 40⁵, which should read 'and all flesh shall see together that the mouth of the LORD hath spoken'. The reliability of God's word is emphasized in the following verses (Isa 40⁶⁻⁸) in the contrast between the steadfastness (not '*goodliness*') of man and the steadfastness of God. The steadfastness of man is non-existent—men are like wild flowers which quickly fade when they are pulled—but the word of God is steadfast and sure, and what He says is firm and reliable.

4⁵. The lofty monotheism of the previous verses and the world-wide missionary hope have gone. So soon do the most glorious visions of men fade, and even man's Vision of God becomes clouded. We turn our eyes from heaven to earth; we talk in terms of what is practicable and what is impracticable; and the glorious fulfilment of all man's hopes is as far away as ever.

4⁶⁻⁸: Back home again

Judah is in exile, far away from Jerusalem. Yahweh promises to restore the scattered remnants of His people into a true Remnant, and through them to restore the fallen glories of Zion-Jerusalem (cf. a similar passage in Zeph 3¹⁹, and especially Ezek 34¹⁶, which with its context may well be the basis of these verses in Micah). The prophet is thinking of Yahweh the shepherd (see Ezek 34) gathering together His scattered flock, some of them lame, some broken by pain and exposure, all of them scattered far and wide. The '*tower of the flock*' (towers for shelter and for the watcher: 2 Chr 26[10], Hab 2[1]) is Ophel (*RV*m), the south-east peak of the temple hill. When the flock is gathered, all the former glory of the kingdom will be established.

4[7]. The word Remnant has already gained a technical significance, since here it is equivalent to '*a strong nation*'. The Remnant is not now simply a surviving residue of a people that has been scattered and destroyed. It is a group, divinely spared and divinely guided, destined to be the means by which the Will of God shall be maintained in a world gone wrong.

4[9-10]: Exile and return

The prophet mocks the people. Why do they cry aloud for help? Have they not got a king and counsellor to guide them? Pain and travail will come upon Jerusalem, but God will ultimately rescue her from her enemies.

4[11-13]: The triumph of Zion

Zion's enemies are ringing her round, but Yahweh has His own plans. His threshing day is near, and the nations are the sheaves for His threshing-floor. The '*iron horn*' (verse 13) does not belong to the imagery of the threshing-floor, but is symbolic of Israel's power and strength in overcoming her enemies. The hoofs of bronze refer to the feet of the oxen that tread out the corn (Deut 25[4]). And all the spoil which the heathen have gathered will be devoted to the Lord. If the Hebrew is correct here and the word 'devoted' has its usual meaning, the prophet is speaking, not of the people of Zion bringing the spoil of the heathen to God as a gift, but utterly and completely destroying it. It is the same word that was used of the destruction of Jericho (Josh 6[18, 24]). But possibly the prophet does not mean that the accumulated booty which the nations have gathered is to be put under the ban and destroyed; possibly the word (*cherem*) is used in a weakened sense, and we have the same picture as in Zechariah 14[14]. Nevertheless, in view of the earlier part of verse 13, the probability is that the prophet was thinking of complete and absolute destruction.

5¹: The city besieged

This verse apparently refers to Jerusalem in a state of siege, and to the humiliation of the king. But the Hebrew is obscure. *RV* takes the first part of the verse as referring to clusters of troops gathering together; the Greek Versions take it as having to do with walls, or with cutting oneself as a sign of mourning.

5²⁻⁴: Born in Bethlehem

There will be an heir of David's line who shall restore the kingdom of David, but it will be greater than ever David's was. The verses are important in Christian tradition because of Matthew 2⁶, where it is said that the chief priests and the scribes quoted this passage and so sent the wise men on to Bethlehem. The quotation in Matthew 2⁶ is loosely rendered, especially the latter part of it. Apparently New Testament writers trusted often to their memories, and were more concerned about the general import of a passage than the precise verbal details.

5². The meaning of the text is 'too little to be among the thousands of Judah'. It is better to omit '*to be*' as an insertion mistakenly made on the analogy of the last line of the verse; we then read 'least among the thousands of Judah'. But here again, when we read '*thousands*' we should not think of numbers, but of small administrative divisions in olden times: e.g. the 'hundreds' of medieval England. Note that a '*not*' is inserted in Matthew 2⁶; this may be due to a misunderstanding of the reading of some minor Greek manuscripts which turn the phrase into a question.

5³ is best regarded as an insertion, the meaning being 'God will surrender the people into exile until the birth of the child, and then all exiles will return.' This verse looks very like a combination of the ideas of Isaiah 7¹⁴⁻¹⁶, 7³, and 10²¹. Here, apparently, Isaiah of Jerusalem was looking forward to the birth of a baby in the near future, and saying that the birth of this child would mark the beginning of a new day for Judah; the young woman conceives now, and by the time her child is old enough to know the difference between right and wrong, the great day will have come. The early Christians,

looking back into the Old Testament for passages which would
help them in their understanding of the Person and Work of
Christ, found enough similarities between Isaiah's situation
and their own to be able to use the prophecy with profit.

5⁴. The reference to '*feed (his flock)*' is the warrant for the
New Testament rendering of '*ruler*' by '*shepherd*'.

Note the avoidance of the word 'king'. The word, of course,
is not always avoided in the Old Testament, but there is a
marked tendency in this direction in the prophetic tradition.
This is especially notable in such a chapter as 2 Samuel 7, the
passage which is the seed-bed out of which spring the Messianic
ideas of a saviour prince of David's line. David is called (2
Sam 7⁸) to be, not 'king', but '*prince*' (*nagid*) over God's
people Israel. But there are other passages which also show
this same tendency. When Hilkiah, Ahikam, Achbor and
Shaphan went to consult the prophetess Huldah, her reply
was not 'Tell the King,' but '*Tell ye the man that sent you
unto me*' (2 Kings 22¹⁵). This reply must have been deliberate,
because all four men were court officials of the first rank; they
were the men next the king, and she must have been fully
aware that Josiah had sent them. Gideon, having rescued the
men of Israel from the Midianites, refuses to allow the people
to make him king: '*I will not rule over you, neither shall my
son rule over you, the* LORD *shall rule over you*' (Judg 8²³).
The young Jotham makes it plain by his allegory of the trees
who went to make themselves a king that only persons of no
worth would aspire to such a position (Judg 9⁸⁻¹⁵). According
to one of the traditions embodied in the Books of Samuel, the
prophet Samuel was against the idea of there being a king
over Israel, because '*the* LORD *your God was your king*' (1
Sam 12¹²), and he regarded the desire of the people for a king
as a sign of their great wickedness. The fact of the matter is
that the great prophetic tradition is that God alone is King,
and to Him alone all honour, all loyalty and all obeisance are
due. And whilst the Jews of later times certainly spoke of
'King Messiah', it is well to remember this tendency to think
of Messiah, not as king in his own right, but as prince of the
Kingdom of God, acting as God's regent on earth. This
attitude arises out of the insistence that God alone rules over
all and that man must have no intruding loyalty.

There is a curious phrase in verse 2: '*whose goings forth*

are from old, from everlasting'. It is a statement that the coming ruler who comes forth out of Bethlehem belongs also to the far distant past. There is an ancient Egyptian writing which speaks of a 'messiah' and says that he is a reincarnation of the Egyptian god Ra and that therefore he can be thought of as belonging to the first generation of mankind. It is a strange thought to be found in the ancient world. What did the Egyptian writer mean? What does the Hebrew prophet mean? To us, who look back through our knowledge of Christ, it would appear that the prophet was speaking a greater truth than he realized. For us the passage means that the Jesus who was born in Bethlehem is our Saviour from before the foundation of the world. The truth we thus maintain is that God's saving grace is available for all mankind every-where, and that there is none that is out of the reach of His love. We also desire to maintain that the Coming of Christ into this world was no sudden decision on the part of God, no sudden complete change of plan, but that He has always been the same, yesterday, today and for ever—always the same Saviour God, active in seeking to win men back to Himself. He has ten thousand different ways of doing it, but He is always doing the same thing. He will do something He has never done before (e.g. the Incarnation), but it will always be of the same pattern. He does this new thing because it is fully in accordance with His behaviour since before the world began.

A prophet is a man who speaks a greater truth than he knows. If we accept that he is speaking the Word of God, there is nothing untoward in supposing that there is an extra more-than-human element in it. The prophet will consciously be speaking what he believes to be the Word of God for one particular occasion. But there will always be a double element in what he says: there will be the application to the particular occasion, which is true for that occasion and may or may not be applicable to another occasion; there will also be the funda-mental truth which is applicable to all occasions. It is in this last sphere that the prophet may be speaking a greater truth than he realizes. The business of the interpreter of the Bible is to disentangle the particular application from the general theme, that is, to seek out what is the temporal and what is the eternal. The next step for the practising Christian is to seek to apply the eternal principle to the particular circum-stances in which he finds himself. This he must do by prayer, by earnest thought, and by consultation with Christians of established experience who may be able to help him toward his own decision.

The fact that in speaking the Word of God the prophet may speak a greater word than he knows is the ground of Christian exegesis of the Bible generally and of the Old Testament in particular. For instance, the famous chapter Isaiah 53 speaks of the triumph of the Servant of the Lord who has suffered unjustly for the sins of the many. It is the general opinion that the prophet is thinking of either an individual or a group. He realizes from his knowledge of the suffering of this individual or group something of the healing power of vicarious suffering. The immediate application is to the promised return from exile and the future restoration of the community in and around Jerusalem. But all Christians see in this chapter a foretelling of the death of Christ. Its truth does not lie in the fact that every detail was fulfilled in His death, though there are Christians who believe that it does. Rather it lies in the fact that the Sacrifice and Death of Christ is a deeper and more complete fulfilment of the vision of the prophet. He saw '*in a mirror darkly*' that which we see more clearly in the humiliation and death of Christ, that which by grace we shall see '*face to face*' hereafter. And yet, he did not see it altogether darkly. There was more to be seen in the vision of truth God gave him, more to be seen than he could clearly read. But we know more of God's saving work in Christ, and we can see much more in his words than he intended. We can see more because, thanks to our living after Christ suffered under Pontius Pilate, we understand a little more clearly the ways of God with men. And here in 5² we have this strange verse in which we can see a reference to the eternal Christ.

5⁵⁻⁶: This means . . .

These two verses are an application of the general prophecy and promise of the previous verses. The application is this. The Assyrian invader is coming and he will trample down our palaces (the ancient Greek and Syriac Versions have 'our land'). But there will be raised up against him seven or eight leaders, and they will drive him out and trample Assyria and all the Mesopotamian valley just as he has trampled down our land. They will deliver us from the Assyrian when he invades us. This (verse 4) is the peace of which the prophet has been speaking.

But what is the historical reference? If the reference is actually to the Assyria of history, then the prophecy was never fulfilled. It is true that Assyria was overrun toward the end of the seventh century B.C. and that the city of Nineveh itself fell in 612 B.C., but this was not due to the efforts of any Judæan prince. It was part of the general collapse of the Assyrian Empire at the death of Asshur-bani-pal in 626 B.C. But the reference to Assyria in verses 5 and 6 may not be to the actual Assyria of history. There are several instances where 'Egypt' and 'Assyria' mean the enemy to the south and west and the enemy to the north-east (Lam 5⁶, Zech 10¹¹, etc., and Ezra 6²² where the reference must be either to Babylonia or Persia). Similarly, in the Book of Jonah, Nineveh is the typical heathen city. It may be, therefore, that the references in 5⁵⁻⁶ are to the heathen generally, and that the passage refers to the overthrow of the heathen powers at the End of Days, the picture with which we are familiar in the apocalypses. The mention of '*seven . . . eight*' is not to be taken as meaning exactly seven or eight, but an indefinite number of moderate dimensions. This is a method of giving a rough estimate, used occasionally in the Old Testament (Amos 1³, Prov 30¹⁸, etc.—three and four; similarly Prov 6¹⁶—six and seven); it is descended from ancient Canaanite literature such as has been found on the site of the ancient Ugarit in Syria.

5⁷⁻⁹: The lion of the Lord

This is another picture of the triumph of the Remnant, or rather two pictures which do not easily fit each other. The second simile, that of the lion, represents the new Jacob-Judah as a destructive adversary of all the nations, forging his way through cattle and sheep, trampling them, tearing them in pieces; no one is able to rescue them from his fury. This is the messianic hope at its most ferocious and vengeful. The first simile is much more difficult to interpret, and there have been many differences of opinion. One type of explanation belongs to that realm of typology which unfortunately is becoming fashionable. It bases the interpretation on Deuteronomy 32², and says that the dew typifies the teaching of God; the meaning therefore is that Israel will be the true teacher of the nations. A reference can then be deduced to Christianity being born out of Judaism and Palestine. Such an interpretation is forced. A more natural explanation is based on the fact that during the summer heat the dew is the only source of moisture for plant-life, and that the fertility of Palestine depended on this and on the refreshing showers of autumn and spring. These are gifts of God and are independent of man. Thus the new Israel is wholly dependent on God's gifts and His grace, and so '*tarrieth not for man, nor waiteth for the sons of men*'. This indeed is true for all who trust in God, and seek in Him their strength and happiness (see Ps 56⁴). This reliance upon God is the basis of the list of the heroes of the faith in Hebrews 11, where the writer has gone through his Bible (the Septuagint) and has picked out those who found their strength in God and not in man, because they believed that God could fulfil the promises He had made, and not only could fulfil them, but would fulfil them. See also Philippians 4¹³ and all references to the '*power of the Spirit*'.

5¹⁰⁻¹⁵: In God alone

These six verses are thought by some to be from Micah of Moresheth-gath, though their scope is somewhat wider than that of the first three chapters of the book. The prophet is here very fierce against all the things to which men pin their faith for safety and greatness, against chariot-horses and their chariots, against walled and fortified cities, against sorcerers and soothsayers, against the images and the stone-pillars which were a feature of all shrines after the Canaanite pattern. It is as though he would sweep away everything else in which men can trust, so that they must perforce trust in God alone.

5¹⁰. The reference is to the chariot-horse; horses were rarely used by the Israelites for riding until later times.

5¹². The modern equivalent of the ancient soothsaying is spiritualism.

5¹³. The stone-pillar was common in Canaan. There were three types: one, a single stone such as that which Jacob set up at Bethel, regarded as the dwelling-place of the god; two, the stone pillar which was accompanied by a wooden pole, the former representing the Baal (the male) and the latter representing the Astarte (the female); three, many stone pillars which were altars for the reception of sacrifices of various types. The Deuteronomic reformation sought to abolish all these, considering them to be (as indeed they almost entirely were) adjuncts of heathen and idolatrous worship.

5¹⁴. The '*Asherim*' were the wooden posts of Canaanite worship. Some used to say that they were always symbols of Astarte, the fertility goddess of Syria and the Near East generally. (The usual spelling in the Hebrew text of 'Astarte' is '*Ashtoreth*', because the scribes inserted the vowels of the word *bosheth* (shame), thereby signifying the idolatrous association.) But it is now known that whilst the wooden post which accompanied the stone-pillar represented Astarte, there was also a goddess named Asherah. There is considerable confusion everywhere in Syria between the three goddesses, Anath (Queen of Heaven), Astarte, and Asherah.

The mention of '*cities*' at the end of the verse is strange. Scholars think that it is a mistake for 'baals' or 'images' or some such word, and indeed such a word would secure a parallel term to '*Asherim*', thus maintaining the repeated parallelisms of the whole passage.

Hezekiah destroyed even the bronze '*serpent that Moses had made*' (2 Kings 18⁴), because the children of Israel worshipped it (see *MHB* 461⁵, also Ps 20⁷). Isaiah had the same kind of thing to say in his day (31¹). The wise man glories in his wisdom (Jer 9²³), the swift man in his speed, and the strong in his strength (Amos 2¹⁴); indeed if there is anything which a man can do better than his fellows, the temptation to trust in it can be well nigh irresistible. Men will trust in anything, everything, for their well-being, their salvation; but particularly in what they can do. It is worth noting that the prophets often argue against idols, not on the ground that nobody can possibly make anything adequate to represent God (as in Isa 40¹⁸, etc.), but on the ground that they are made by man. From this point of view, their attack on idols is a particular instance of the general warning against trusting in our own works of whatever type they may be. Man must trust in God alone; that is, he must have faith in God alone (*MHB* 359).

6¹⁻⁵: Yahweh *v.* Israel

These verses embody Yahweh's case against Israel. The prophet calls to the mountains and the hills that surround Jerusalem. He calls to the very foundations of the earth. What has Yahweh done to Israel that Israel should be weary of Him? Yahweh's deeds for Israel have all been mighty, righteous, saving deeds. Israel has no case.

6². '*ye enduring*'. This cannot really be got out of the Hebrew. Some scholars suggest that there is an error for 'give ear, ye . . .', thus making the second half of the line parallel to the first half.

6⁵. Balak hired Balaam to curse Israel, but Balaam blessed Israel abundantly, because it is God who fixes curses and blessings (Num 23⁸) and Balaam could reverse nothing even if he would (Num 23²⁰).

6⁵. '*Remember "from Shittim to Gilgal"* '. The phrase '*from Shittim to Gilgal*' looks like an ancient phrase, pregnant with traditional meaning. And indeed this is so. Shittim was the last camp east of Jordan, and Gilgal was the first camp west of Jordan. Between Shittim and Gilgal there was the crossing of Jordan, the entrance to the Promised Land (Josh 3¹, 4²⁰). Further '*the righteous acts of the* LORD' are His mighty saving acts, those wondrous deeds which He accomplished on behalf of the sons of Israel through the years, but particularly those mighty deeds which were associated with Exodus, those stirring events which led to God's choice of Israel on Sinai to be His people, His peculiar (that is, special) people. This motif is found everywhere—e.g. '*Then Samuel took a stone, and set it between Mizpah and Shen, and called the name of it Ebenezer, saying, Hitherto hath the LORD helped us*' (1 Sam 7¹²), *MHB* 417, Isa 63⁷⁻¹⁴; and the historical psalms, 78, 105, 106, 107, especially 135 and 136, which seem to be careful and elaborate attempts to make sure that the people really did know and understand the significance of their past history, that it was all the story of the great things which Yahweh had done for them. To us who live after the Saving Work of Christ, and who can say something of the working of the Holy Spirit since that first Christian Pentecost, there is a yet grander story to be told of God's unfailing mercies. The Israelites had little excuse for being weary of God and for turning away from Him; we of the Christian Era have still less excuse.

6⁶⁻⁸: True religion

What is it that Yahweh, the high God, requires? animals, yearling calves? rams by thousand? gushers of oil by the thousand? first-born sons? What God requires is right conduct, delight in being faithful, and true humility in His presence.

6⁷. The natural meaning of this verse is that the sacrifice of the first-born son is the most precious and costly sacrifice of all. It would appear that at one time the first-born was sacrificed in Israel in times of special peril, and that this sacrifice was regarded as being peculiarly effective (2 Kings 3²⁷). Both Ahaz and Manasseh sacrificed their sons (2 Kings 16³, 21⁶), but Josiah took steps to make such sacrifices impossible for ever (2 Kings 23¹⁰). He did not succeed, because there was a revival of the custom in the last desperate days of Jerusalem when the doom of exile was hanging heavy over the city (Jer 19⁴⁻⁶, Ezek 16²⁰, 20²⁶). The repeated prohibitions throughout the generations show how common and deep-rooted the custom was. It is generally held that the story of Abraham's willingness to sacrifice Isaac and the substitution of the ram is a reflection of the prohibition of such human sacrifices.

6⁸. '*to do justly*'. The meaning is to keep God's justice. Just as it is our duty as citizens to maintain the Queen's Justice in her/our land, so it was the duty of the devout Israelite to keep King Yahweh's justice in His land.

In the phrase '*to love mercy*' the word is *chesed*, and the meaning is to delight in keeping the covenant with God in loving loyalty (see note on Hos 6⁵).

God requires ultimately nothing that men can bring Him, but men themselves. He requires no gifts from us except the gift of ourselves. There was a time when men thought they had to make gifts to God in order to placate Him and persuade Him to turn to them in favour. We know that man cannot do anything to make God turn to Him, for the simple reason that His face is always turned toward us in love. He loves us with an everlasting love and has loved us since the foundation of the world. There is no need of any sacrifice to appease Him, and no ritual acts can make Him more pre-disposed to us than He already is. What God requires is right conduct from man, not only the righteousness which is of the law (that is, not only morality), but that righteousness which reaches out far beyond any legal statement of it, the 'righteousness' which involves seeking and saving the lost (see note on Amos 2⁶), which is concerned with him that hath no helper. What God requires is faithfulness to the covenant, loyal love and devotion, that 'leal-love' which fulfils our share in what is necessary to maintain the right relationship between God and man. For religion consists of more than morality and of more than performing ritual acts in proper fashion at stated time. Religion consists in a right relationship with God. On His side it is Grace (His unfailing, undeserved love) that is the basis of the relationship; on our side it is humble trust. This is why the prophet concludes His recital of the essence of true religion with '*and walk humbly with thy God*'. To say that God requires ultimately nothing that men can bring does not mean that men ought not to worship Him. Worship is necessary for man, because it is the outward expression of true humility before God, of that humble trust which is essential. It is when worship ceases to be this that it is a hindrance and not a help; so long as it is the outcome of true and humble conscious devotion to God, it can and does strengthen those bonds which bind God and man together through Christ. Worship is also necessary because man should be full of praise and thankfulness to God; but as soon as the aim of hymns and songs and music generally becomes aesthetic, it is the time to beware. It is doubtless better that music in worship should be good rather than bad, whatever exactly 'good' and 'bad' may mean at any particular stage of musical development, but the ultimate question is: Is this music the expression of true faith and piety? As soon as music ceases to be that, it may become a hindrance to true religion, and not a help toward it. All this applies to any and every form of worship.

All forms of true and devout worship are also a help in the cause of true religion. This is not because they make or encourage any change in God. There is no change possible in God that will make Him love us any more than He already does, and no change possible in Him that will make Him more ready to forgive the repentant sinner. The forms of worship, if truly devout, are a help in the cause of true religion because they can change us, the worshippers. By the deliberate expression of faith, repentance and humble trust, we make ourselves more fit to be 'channels of grace', instruments through which the Holy Spirit can work.

6⁹⁻¹⁶: Sin of the city and its punishment

The prophet arraigns the city for its wickedness, the cheating of the business men, the rapacity of the rich, the lies of the inhabitants as a whole. The penalty is hunger, poverty, death, failure of harvests, destruction and scorn.

The Hebrew text in many of these verses is uncertain, and much use has to be made of the ancient versions (see *RSV*) if we are to make the passage intelligible.

6⁹. '*and the man of wisdom will see thy name*' is probably an insertion into the original. In any case read '*fear*' (*RSV*) for '*see*'. For '*hear ye the rod*', read '*hear, O tribe and assembly of the city*' (*RSV*).

6¹⁰. 'Can I forget the treasures (gained by) wickedness in the house of the wicked?'

6¹¹. 'Shall I treat as pure (*RSV* "*acquit*") the man with wicked scales?'

6¹³. 'And so I have begun to smite you'.

6¹⁴. The word translated '*humiliation*' is unknown; this is the guess of the Vulgate. The ancient Syriac thought it meant 'dysentery'; *RSV* has '*hunger*'. Much depends on whether the next word is to be translated 'in thy midst' or 'in thy inside'.

6¹⁶. '*the statutes of Omri*', the father of Ahab, are the customs and religious errors of Israel a hundred years before the time of Amos, Hosea and Micah, the Baal worship against which Elijah and Elisha fought, and all the immoralities of that cult. For '*my people*', it is better to follow the Greek Version and read 'peoples'.

The prophet knows that God demands a proper standard of morality in business and fair dealing between buyer and seller. The passage is a tirade against all those who seek to get rich quickly and are not very particular about the means they adopt. Today in our own country there is little actual cheating of the precise type which the prophet condemns; her majesty's inspectors of weights and measures prevent this. But it is probable that the prophet would condemn all exploitation of the public, all restrictive practices, whether by employer or by employee, all price rings, and every person whoever he be who seeks to take out more than he puts in.

7^{1-6}: Jerusalem's lament

Everything has gone. The harvest field is swept clean. There is not an honest man left in the city, and no man can trust another; '*a man's enemies are the men of his own house*'.

7^1. Dr George Adam Smith translates this verse 'Woe is me, for I am become like sweepings of harvest, like gleanings of the vintage', and this makes much better sense than either *RV* or *RSV*. Instead of '*my soul desireth the firstripe fig*', follow *RV*m or *RSV*.

7^3. '*the prince asketh*' is by no means clear. The Syriac Version added 'gold'; Dr George Adam Smith has 'the prince makes requisition'. Both readings are sound interpretations, though we could run the two phrases together and read '*the prince and the judge ask for bribes*' (*RSV*). The prophet pictures them all busy at work, each for his own personal gain, and together weaving a pattern of woe.

7^4. '*brier*', i.e. 'a brier patch' or 'a thorn thicket' (G. A. Smith). The meaning of the phrase 'the day of thy watchmen' is: the day of disaster which your prophets foresaw. The figure of the watchmen is a well-used metaphor for the prophet.

Here is the climax of individualism, of every man looking out for himself and seeking his own personal welfare. This is possible in any type of society, though men can always see such weaknesses in the type of society they themselves do not favour. It may be that one type of society conduces to selfish behaviour more than another, but the real problem in every society is that of the individual. In primitive society there was the witch-doctor, whose primary duty was to ensure that the supernatural powers were used for the good of the tribe as a whole, and to prevent any individual from using these powers for his own advantage and against any other member of the community. And all down the ages there have had to be restraints upon the individual to prevent self-centred behaviour. The whole of human history could be written as the story of successive failures to curb the selfishness of individual men and separate nations. Perhaps there will come a day when it is realized that the real problem of society, indeed the real problem of the comity of nations, is the problem of the individual man and the need of conversion. The heart and will of man must be controlled. How is it to be controlled? By law? If so, by what law? If the control is to be exercised from within, then how is this to be accomplished? Can education do it? And if so, what sort of education? If there is to be a radical change in the hearts and intentions of men, then how is this to be accomplished? The Christian answer is 'by a complete change of heart', by conversion. This does not mean that the Christian should leave politics alone, or that he should take no interest in the management of human affairs. He must do this, and he must show himself a Christian in all these affairs. There can be nothing more disastrous than for Christian people either to contract out of public affairs, or to modify Christian principles so that their attitude is no different from that of those who make no Christian confession. But at the same time we must work unceasingly and energetically for that complete difference of attitude which marks the ultimate difference between the Christian and the non-Christian.

7⁷⁻¹⁰: My hope is in God

Israel may fall, but she will rise again. The enemy that jeered at her on the grounds that she had been deserted by her God, will be covered with confusion and trampled in the muddy streets.

7⁹. for '*righteousness*', read '*deliverance*' (*RSV*). There are very many instances in the prophets and in the psalms where the Hebrew word commonly translated 'righteousness' should be rendered 'salvation, victory, deliverance'. The word does not mean right ethical conduct, so much as to be in the right; or, if the word should be thought of as indicating 'conforming to the norm', then in the minds of the prophets it means conforming to God's ways and character. Thus it can mean, not only sound ethical conduct, but reaching out beyond that to seek and to save that which is lost. So the corresponding verb, used often in the Pauline writings and translated 'justify', means rather cleaning the slate of the past and starting afresh. It is generally agreed that 'justify' does not mean 'make righteous'. It is commonly said that it means 'treat as righteous'. The word can be better understood, however, if we think of God clearing away all past sins, wiping them out, on the basis of our true repentance and faith in Him, so that we can make a new start, unhampered by the weight of our past; we are 'put right' with God. The whole group of words (righteousness, justification, justify) is better understood as having a personal reference and being descriptive of a relationship, than in ethical terms.

The prophet thinks of the people as repentant and looking away to God for a happy issue out of all their woes. But everything depends upon the kind of 'looking away' to God. There is a type of looking away to God which is actually the avoidance of responsibility—a sitting with folded hands expecting God to do everything, expecting God to put His arm through the sky and accomplish His purposes independently of men's thoughts and deeds. This type of other-worldliness is dangerous and even deadly. It gives a free hand to all the powers of evil and to all the selfishness of man. The true and proper way of looking away to God is to look to Him for inspiration, guidance and strength, to look to Him for the standards by which we may judge conduct, the standards by which we can order our lives, and the strength by which we do this ordering. We are not to be spectators of the emancipation of the world, watching the struggles from the side-lines. Our place is in the midst of the struggle, but guided and strengthened by Him. The true attitude is that in Hebrews 12[1f]: 'let us run with endurance the race that is set before us, looking unto Jesus, the author and perfecter of our faith.'

7[8]. God will be a light in the midst of darkness. If this is thought of as a gleam to follow, there are two ways of following.

Most people think that following the gleam means following the gleam back to its source, using it as a guide to bring us to our heavenly home. This is a sound interpretation of the picture, since we all 'trust by His good pleasure, safely to arrive at home'. But there is another way, a better way, of following the gleam. This is to follow the gleam as it goes out into the darkness. I prefer this interpretation, for instance, in the phrase *'light to the Gentiles'*, though probably here both ideas are combined. The servant is to be a *'light to the Gentiles'* to spread God's salvation to the end of the earth. But there is also the hope that all the nations will be guided to God's holy hill. It is better to think of following the gleam out into the darkness, since the mission of the Christian is not primarily to save his own soul, but to be the servant of the Lord to bring others to Him. Indeed, *'he that saveth his soul, shall lose it'*. It is this saying which puts the emphasis on following the gleam out into the darkness for the saving of others, rather than following the gleam back to its source in order to save ourselves.

7¹¹⁻¹³: The exiles return

What a day it will be when the walls of Jerusalem are rebuilt, and when all the exiles return! The boundary of the city will have to be extended. By way of contrast, the heathen world will be desolate because of the wickedness of its inhabitants.

7¹¹. for *'decree'*, read 'boundary' (*RV*m).

7¹². the Hebrew has 'besieged cities' and 'siege', but in each case it is better to follow the Greek Version and read *'Egypt'*.

7¹³. This verse must refer to the whole Gentile world and not to the land of Canaan. It may possibly refer to the land of Canaan as distinct from Jerusalem, but this is less likely.

It used to be thought that verse 12 referred to all the gentile nations coming to Jerusalem, but it is not now thought to do so. It is believed generally that the reference is to the exiles of the post-exilic period, the Diaspora. Verse 13 reflects the ancient opinion that the land shared the penalty of the sins of its inhabitants in lack of fruitfulness.

7¹⁴⁻²⁰: A final prayer

The prophet prays for renewed blessing and guidance, for God to be a shepherd to His people as in the old days when He led them through the wilderness from Egypt to Canaan. May the nations see the new deliverance, be ashamed of all their boasted might, and come humbly in dread to God! Yahweh is a pardoning God, casting the sins of repentant Israel away out of sight, steadfast and loyal to the covenant which He made with the Israelites of old time.

7¹⁴. '*feed*' is not vivid enough, and '*rule*' (*AV*m and *RV*m) is here a mistaken interpretation; read '*shepherd*' (*RSV*). The '*rod*' is the shepherd's staff (Ps 23⁴). '*In the forest in the midst of Carmel*' makes no sense. The '*forest*' is rough country, trees, precipices, dangerous and unlovely, and the word '*Carmel*' should be translated, not regarded as a proper name. Read '*which dwell alone in a forest in the midst of a garden land*' (*RSV*), which probably means: living desolate in the barren Judaean hill country with the fertile lowlands to the north and west. The reference to Bashan and Gilead, both pasture lands east of Jordan, is the old nostalgic allusion to the glorious days of the desert (see note on Hos 2¹⁴).

7¹⁶⁻¹⁷. It is best to treat these verses as part of the prayer, 'may the nations see . . . .'.

7¹⁸. For '*passeth by the transgression*' read 'passes over the rebellion'. For '*mercy*', read 'steadfast love' as often elsewhere. The reference is to that steadfast love which God retains for the people of His covenant, the basis of His continued saving grace throughout the generations.

7¹⁹. Not '*their sins*', but 'our sins', following all the ancient translations.

7²⁰. Follow *RV*m, 'thou wilt show faithfulness' (omit 'thy'; it is not in the original Hebrew). The names of their forefathers, Jacob and Abraham, stand for all their descendants who are within the covenant.

For references to Yahweh as the Shepherd of Israel, see the note on Amos 7¹⁴. The last three verses form the core of

Hebrew religion as the preparation for the Gospel. Yahweh is a pardoning God and there is none like Him (*MHB* 356); and now that '*the middle wall of partition*' (Eph 2¹⁴) is broken down in Christ, His pardon is free to every repentant sinner the whole world over. The reason for this continued offer is to be found in His steadfast love (Hebrew *chesed*), His determined faithfulness to His covenant with His people. '*If we are faithless, he abideth faithful*' (2 Tim 2¹³). This is why there is always hope. When men turn to Him in humble faith, He once more shows His compassion (*RV* '*he will turn again*' is misleading; this is the Hebrew idiom for 'he will again have compassion'). God's face is never turned away from us, and not all the sins of man can destroy His steadfast love. When we turn to Him, our sins are put out of sight, trodden under foot, thrown into the depths of the sea, cast away so that they no longer obtrude between God and us. This is the message of salvation which we preach; it is a full and free forgiveness in Christ, conditional only on repentance and faith.

Bibliography

Amos

The Book of the Twelve Prophets, Vol. I, by George Adam Smith (Hodder & Stoughton).

The Minor Prophets, Vol. I, by R. F. Horton. (Century Bible, T. C. & E. C. Jack).

Amos, Parts I and II, by Norman H. Snaith (Epworth Press).

The Book of Amos, translated into colloquial English by Theodore H. Robinson (National Adult School Union).

The Books of Joel and Amos, by S. R. Driver and H. C. O. Lanchester (Cambridge Bible for Schools, Cambridge University Press).

Hosea

The Book of the Twelve Prophets, Vol. I, by George Adam Smith (Hodder and Stoughton).

The Minor Prophets, Vol. I, by R. F. Horton (Century Bible, T. C. & E. C. Jack).

Mercy and Sacrifice, by Norman H. Snaith (S.C.M. Press).

The Book of Hosea, translated into colloquial English by J. W. Povah (National Adult School Union).

Hosea, by T. K. Cheyne (Cambridge Bible for Schools, Cambridge University Press).

Two Hebrew Prophets, Studies in Hosea and Ezekiel, by H. Wheeler Robinson (Lutterworth Press).

Micah

The Book of the Twelve Prophets, Vol. I, by George Adam Smith (Hodder and Stoughton).

The Minor Prophets, Vol. I, by R. F. Horton (Century Bible, T. C. & E. C. Jack).

The Book of Micah, by T. K. Cheyne (Cambridge Bible for Schools, Cambridge University Press).

For Reference

Not to be taken from this room